W9-AZP-449

KAREN BROWN'S

Italian
Country Inns & Itineraries

OTHER KAREN BROWN TITLES

Austrian Country Inns & Castles

California Country Inns & Itineraries

English Country Bed & Breakfasts

English, Welsh & Scottish Country Hotels & Itineraries

French Country Bed & Breakfasts

French Country Inns & Itineraries

German Country Inns & Itineraries

Irish Country Inns

Italian Country Bed & Breakfasts

Italian Country Inns & Itineraries

Portuguese Country Inns & Pousadas

Scandinavian Country Inns & Manors

Spanish Country Inns & Paradors

Swiss Country Inns & Chalets

KAREN BROWN'S

Italian
Country Inns & Itineraries

Written by

CLARE BROWN

Sketches by

Barbara Tapp

Karen Brown's Country Inn Series

Editors: Karen Brown, Clare Brown, June Brown, Nicole Franchini, Iris Sandilands
Technical support: William H. Brown III; Aide-de-camp: William H. Brown
Illustrations: Barbara Tapp; Cover Art: Gerardo Esposito-Felix; Maps: Cassell Design

Written in cooperation with Town and Country - Hillsdale Travel, San Mateo, CA

Copyright © 1985, 1986, 1988, 1992 by Karen Brown's Guides

*All rights reserved. This book or parts thereof may not be reproduced in
any form without obtaining written permission from the publisher Travel Press:*

Karen Brown's Guides
Post Office Box 70
San Mateo, CA 94401
tel: 415-342-9117

Distributed by The Globe Pequot Press, 138 West Main Street, Chester, CT 06412

Library of Congress Cataloging-in-Publication Data

Brown, Clare.
    Karen Brown's Italian country inns & itineraries / written by
Clare Brown ; sketches by Barbara Tapp.
       p. cm. -- (Karen Brown's country inn series)
    Rev. ed. of: Italian country inns & villas. 3rd rev. ed. c1988
    Includes index.
    ISBN 0-930328-05-1 : $14.95
    1. Hotels, taverns, etc. --Italy--Guide-books. 2. Italy-
-Description and travel--1975- --Guide-books. I. Brown, Clare.
Italian country inns & villas. II. Title. III. Series
TX907.5.I8B76 1992
647.944501--dc20
                                     91-41281
                                         CIP

To My Best Friend, Bill

With Love and Gratitude for

Many Miles of Memories

Contents

Foreword

As we go to press with this fourth edition of *Italian Country Inns & Itineraries*, we are pleaseed to include 32 new inns to make your holiday even more special. These additions are some of the most charming small hotels in Italy - many of which are rarely found in other travel guides. A few of these new hotels are ones we happened upon while combing the backroads, others are recommendations from hoteliers, but some of our favorites are those you found and shared with us. Not only is this guide strengthened by your suggestions for new hotels, but also by your criticisms. We have dropped hotels that did not maintain the standards of comfort, hospitality and charm we want you to experience in your travels. Thank you for sharing your adventures - we appreciate your taking the time to write or call. We promise to always inspect every hotel we recommend and, with your help, continue to present you with the finest small hotels throughout Europe.

Introduction

Of all the countries in the world, none is more magical than Italy: truly a tourist's paradise - a traveller's dream destination. No one could be so blasé that within Italy's narrow boot there would not be something to tantalize their fancy. For the archaeologist, there are some of the most fascinating and perfectly preserved ancient monuments existing today - just begging to be explored. For the gourmet, there is probably the best food in the world. For the outdoorsman, there are towering mountains to conquer and magnificent ski slopes to sample. For the lover of art, the museums are bursting with the genius of Italy's sons such as Michelangelo, Leonardo da Vinci, and Raphael. For the architect, Italy is a school of design - you are surrounded by the ancient buildings whose perfection has inspired the styles of today. For the history buff, Italy is a joy of wonders - her cities are veritable living museums where you are surrounded by the ghosts of Caesar. For the wine connoisseur, Italy produces an unbelievable selection of wine whose quality is unsurpassed. For the adventurer, Italy has intriguing medieval walled villages tucked away in every part of the country. For the beach buff, Italy's lakes and islands hold promise of some of the most elegant resorts in the world. For the religious pilgrim, Italy is the cradle of much of the world's faith and home of some of the world's greatest saints. The miracle of Italy is that all these treasures come "packaged" in a gorgeous country of majestic mountains, misty lakes, idyllic islands, wonderful walled villages and gorgeous cities. Plus, the climate is ideal and the people warm and gracious. Italy is a perfect destination.

ABOUT THIS GUIDE

This guide is written with two main objectives: to describe the most romantic small hotels throughout Italy and to "tie" these hotels together with itineraries that include enough details so the traveller can plan his own holiday.

This introduction explains how to use the guide and also touches upon what to expect while travelling. After the introduction comes the main part of the guide which is divided into two sections. The first section outlines itineraries with sightseeing suggestions along the way and a hotel featured for each night's stay. The second section of the book has two parts. First is a complete list of hotels we have personally inspected, appearing alphabetically by town with a description, an illustration, and pertinent information provided for each. Second is a list of hotels recommended by our readers. The hotels featured in our guide vary tremendously: some are deluxe, grand hotels fit for a king and very expensive; others are quite simple little cottages tucked away in remote hamlets that are less expensive. We include them all if they have "personality", charm and an antique ambiance. There are a few hotels which are included that do not quite live up to the criterion of "old-world-charm": the reason they have been included is because in their particular area there just were no "perfect" choices, and since you might need a place to stay, we tried to find the very best possibility.

CURRENT

You will need a transformer plus an adapter if you plan to use an American-made electrical appliance in Italy. The voltage is usually 220, but sometimes it varies and is 115 or 125. Check with the manager of the hotel before plugging anything into an electrical outlet. Frequently the larger hotels can loan you a properly adapted electric hairdryer.

DRIVING

DRIVER'S LICENSE: Although it is not mandatory, it is a good idea to obtain an international driver's license before driving in Italy. Should you have any problems along the way, it is more efficient to show your international card which is easily understood overseas.

GASOLINE: Gasoline is very expensive so plan ahead and budget this as part of your trip if you are driving. If you purchase a car in Europe and it is registered in a country other than Italy, you can buy gas discount coupons at the border.

ROADS: The Italian roads are nothing short of spectacular. You will discover some of the finest highways in the world. In fact, the Italians are absolute geniuses when it comes to their engineering feats (which actually is not such a surprising fact when you think what a fantastic road system the Romans built two thousand years ago). Nothing seems to daunt the engineers. You would think the mountains are of clay instead of solid rock, the way the roads tunnel through them. Sometimes a roadway will be seemingly suspended in mid- air, as it bridges a mountain crevasse.

TOLL ROADS: Italy has a network of super expressways that draws the whole country into an easily manageable destination by car. Once you are on the toll roads the miles whip by and you can go quickly from almost any area of Italy to another most efficiently. However, be forewarned: these toll roads are very expensive. It seems that about every half hour a toll station appears and you owe several dollars. But, every cent is well spent when you consider the alternative of creeping along within a maze of trucks and buzzing motorcycles taking forever to go only a few miles. Use the toll roads for the major distances you need to cover, and then choose the small roads when you wish to meander leisurely through the countryside.

The toll roads are mystifying until you learn the system - even then it is confusing because just when you think you have the operation "down pat" you will find it varies slightly. But this is the most common routine: first follow the green expressway signs toward the toll road. Sometimes these signs begin miles from the expressway so be patient and continue the game of "follow the sign". Each entrance to the expressway handles traffic going in both directions. As you enter into the toll gate there is usually a red button you push and a card pops out of a slot. After going through the toll station you choose the direction you want to go. Leaving the expressway there will be a toll station where your ticket will be collected and you will pay according to how many miles travelled.

ROAD SIGNS: Before starting on the road prepare yourself by learning the international driving signs so that you can obey all the rules of the road and avoid the embarrassment of heading the wrong way down a small street or parking in a forbidden area. There are several basic sign shapes. The triangular signs warn that there is danger ahead. The circular signs indicate compulsory rules and information. The square signs give information concerning telephones, parking, camping, etc. Some of the more common signs are listed below:

| No entry for pedestrians | No animals | No entry for all motor vehicles | End of no overtaking | No overtaking for lorries | End of no overtaking |

| Danger! Level crossing | Low-flying aircraft | Falling rocks | Cross-wind | Quayside or river bank | Two-way traffic |

| Give way | Slippery road | Uneven road | Steep hill - descent | Tunnel | Opening bridge |

| End of all restrictions | Halt sign | Halt sign | Customs | No stopping | No parking/waiting |

| Mechanical help | Filling station | Telephone | Camping site | Caravan site | Youth hostel |

| All vehicles prohibited | No entry for all vehicles | No right turn | No U-turns | No entry for motorcars | No overtaking |

| Road works | Loose chippings | Level crossing with barrier | Level crossing without barrier | Maximum speed limit | End of speed limit |

| Traffic signals ahead | Pedestrians | Children | Animals | Wild animals | Other dangers |

| Intersection with non-priority road | Merging traffic from left | Merging traffic from right | Road narrows | Road narrows at left | Road narrows at right |

Introduction   5

FOOD and DRINK

It is almost impossible to get a bad meal in Italy. Italians themselves love to eat and seem to make dining a social occasion to be with family and friends, so the restaurants are filled not only with tourists but with the Italians who dawdle at the tables long after the meal is over, chatting and laughing with perhaps a glass of wine or a last cup of coffee.

You will soon get in the spirit of the game of deciding which kind of restaurant to choose for your next meal - and the selection is immense, all the way from the simple family trattoria where mama is cooking in the kitchen to the most elegant of gourmet restaurants with world renowned chefs. Whichever you choose, you will not be disappointed.

The Italians are artists when it comes to pasta, seen on every menu and prepared in endless, fascinating, delicious ways. Wine of course is served with every meal. You rarely see an Italian family eating without their bottle of wine on the table. Unless you are a true wine connoisseur I suggest the regional wines. If you ask your waiter to assist you with the choice, you will flatter him and discover many superb wines. Some of the most popular wines which you will see on the Italian menus are: CHIANTI, a well-known wine produced in the Tuscany area south of Florence; MARSALA, a golden sweet wine from Sicily; SOAVE, a superb light wine produced near Venice; ORVIETO, a semi-sweet wine from the Umbria area near Assisi and EST EST EST, a beautiful semi-sweet wine produced near Rome. The story that I heard about the last wine, Est Est Est, is lots of fun and perhaps even true. It seems that many years ago a wealthy nobleman was travelling south, and, being a true gourmet both of food and drink, he sent his servant before him to pick out all the best places to eat and drink along the way. When the servant neared Rome he found such a divine wine that all he could relay back to his master was EST EST EST, which students of Latin will remember means Yes Yes Yes. And the wine is definitely still "Yes Yes Yes" as are most that you will enjoy drinking in Italy.

HOTELS - BASIS FOR SELECTION

This guide does not try to appeal to everyone. It is definitely prejudiced - each hotel included is one we have seen and liked. It might be a splendid villa elegantly positioned overlooking one of Italy's romantic lakes or a simple little chalet snuggled high in a mountain meadow. But there is a common denominator - they all have charm. Therefore, if you too prefer to travel spending your nights in romantic old villas, appealing little chalets, dramatic medieval castles, ancient monasteries, converted peasants' cottages and gorgeous palaces, we are kindred souls, you can follow the paths we have suggested and each night will be an adventure.

For some of you, cost will not be a factor if the hotel is outstanding. For others, budget will guide your choices. The appeal of a simple little inn with rustic wooden furniture will beckon some, while the glamour of ornate ballrooms dressed with crystal chandeliers and gilded mirrors will appeal to others. What we have tried to do is to indicate what each hotel has to offer, and describe the setting, so that you can make the choice to suit your own preferences and holiday. We feel if you know what to expect, you will not be disappointed, so we have tried to be candid and honest in our appraisals. Also, some hotels are ideal for children while others are definitely adult oriented. We have indicated these special situations under the hotel descriptions.

HOTELS - COST

The price for a room in Italy has soared. Even simple places to stay seem desperately over-priced. This is due both to inflation and the fact that the dollar is weak in relationship to the lire. However, if you study carefully the rates given in the back of this guide, you can still find a few bargains available and can plan your trip using one of the less expensive hotels as your "hub" from which to venture out each day.   Because hotels are so expensive, we have published *Italian Country Bed & Breakfasts* which makes an ideal companion to this guide.   The maps in both are similar, making it easy to choose a place to stay from either book.   Not only can you save money by sometimes opting for a bed and breakfast for a night's accommodation, but also enjoy the experience of staying where you have the opportunity to know your host and fellow guests.

HOTELS - CREDIT CARDS

Many small hotels do not accept credit cards. Those hotels which do accept "plastic payment" are indicated in the hotel description section using the following abbreviations: AX - American Express, VS - Visa, MC - Master Charge, DC - Diner's Club, or simply - All major.

HOTELS - DECOR

Hotels usually reflect a rather formal, sometimes fussy ambiance. In a few instances (which we note in the hotel descriptions) the hotels display a country cozy mood, but this is not the norm. When antiques are used, they are frequently the fancy, gilded variety.

HOTELS - HOW TO INTERPRET THE RATE

In the hotel reference section in the back of the book each hotel will show a rate which will reflect the approximate cost for two persons including tax, service and continental breakfast. There are a few hotels where breakfast and one other meal (either lunch or dinner) is included in the rate and, if so, this too is noted. Please use the rates given only as a general ballpark guide because each hotel has such a wide range of price possibilities that it is impossible to project with complete accuracy. Also, each year there is some inflation. However, the lire price given will help you anticipate what the approximate cost will be. When you begin to plan your holiday, check with your bank to see the current exchange rate. Hopefully the dollar will become stronger and travelling in Italy will again become a bargain.

HOTELS - HOW TO ECONOMIZE

For those of you who want to squeeze the most value out of each night's stay, we have several suggestions:

1) Travel off season - spring and fall are usually lovely in Italy and the hotels often have bargain rates.

2) Ask for a room without a private bathroom - many hotels have very nice rooms, usually with a washbasin in the room, but with the bathroom "down the hall".

3) Ask if there is a weekly rate - frequently hotels will offer a price break for guests staying a week or more. If travelling with children, ask if there is a special family suite at a lesser price than separate rooms.

4) Supplement your hotel accommodations with a few nights in a bed and breakfast chosen from *Karen Brown's Italian Country Bed & Breakfasts*.

5) Ask about rates with meals included - if staying for three days or longer, many hotels offer a special rate including meals: MAP (Modified American Plan) means two meals a day are included, AP (American Plan) means three meals a day are included.

6) Last, but not least, is the most important way to save money. Stay out in the countryside instead of in the cities. We cannot stress enough how much more value you receive when you avoid the cities - especially the tourist centers such as Rome, Florence, Milan and Venice. Of course stay right in the heart of town if you are not watching your budget, but if you are trying to squeeze the greatest value from your lire, choose hotels in the countryside and take side trips to visit the pricey tourist centers.

HOTELS - RESERVATIONS

People frequently ask, "Do I need a hotel reservation?" The answer really depends on how flexible you want to be, how tight your time schedule is, in which season you are travelling, and how disappointed you would be if your first choice is unavailable.

It is not unusual for the major tourist cities to be completely sold out during the peak season of June through September. Be forewarned: hotel space in Rome, Florence, Milan and Venice is really at a premium and unless you don't mind taking your chances on a last-minute cancellation or staying on the outskirts of town, make a reservation. Space in the countryside is a little easier. However, if you have your heart set on some special little inn, you certainly should reserve as soon as your travel dates are firm. Reservations are confining. Most hotels will want a deposit to hold your room and frequently refunds are difficult should you change your plans - especially at the last minute. So it is a double bind: making reservations locks you into a solid framework, but without reservations you might be stuck with accommodations you do not like. During the height of the tourist season, some small hotels will only accept reservations for a minimum of three or more nights. However, do not give up because almost all of the hotels which have this policy will take a last-minute booking for a shorter period of time if you call along the way and there is space. For those who like the security blanket of having each night pre-planned so that once you leave home you do not have to worry about where to rest your head, several options for making reservations are listed below:

TRAVEL AGENT: A travel agent can be of great assistance - particularly if your own time is valuable. A knowledgeable agent can handle all of the details of your holiday and "tie" them all together for you in a neat little package including hotel reservations, airline tickets, boat tickets, train reservations, ferry schedules, theater tickets, etc. For your airline tickets there will be no service fee, but most travel agencies make a charge for their other services. The best advice is to talk with your local agent. Be frank about how much you want to spend and ask exactly what he can do for you and what the charges will be. Although the travel agency in your town might not be familiar with all the little places in this guide, since many are so tiny that they appear in no other major sources, loan them your book - it is written as a guide for travel agents as well as for individual travellers.

LETTER: If you start early, you can write directly to the hotels and request exactly what you need. Clearly state the following: number of people in your party; how many rooms you desire; whether you want a private bathroom; date of arrival and date of departure; ask rate per night and if a deposit is needed. When you receive a reply, send the deposit requested and ask for a receipt. Note: When corresponding with Italy be sure to spell out the month. Do not use numbers since in Europe they reverse our system - such as 6/9 means September 6, not June 9. Allow six weeks for an answer - mail to Italy is very slow. Although most hotels can understand a letter written in English, you will find on page 253 a letter written in Italian with an English translation. Photocopy it and use it for your actual request letters.

TELEPHONE: Our preference in making reservations is to call direct. The cost is minimal if you direct dial and you can have your answer immediately. If space is not available, you can then decide on an alternate. Ask your local operator when to call for the lowest rates. Also consider what time it is in Italy when you call (even the most gracious of owners are sometimes a bit grouchy when awakened at 3am). Basically, the system is to dial 011 (the international code) 39 (Italy code). Compose these five numbers then dial the city code (dropping the 0 if dialing from the United States) and the hotel telephone number which appears under the hotel listings. Almost all of the hotels have someone who speaks English. There are a few exceptions and when very little English is spoken, we have tried to indicate this under the hotel's description. The best chance for finding the owner or manager who speaks English is to call when it is late afternoon in Italy.

FAX: If you have access to a fax machine, this is another efficient way to reach a hotel. The majority of hotels in Italy now have fax numbers which we have listed in the back of the book under each hotel listing. Again, be sure to be specific as to your arrival and departure dates, number in your party, and what type of room you want. And, of course, be sure to include your fax number for their response.

U.S. REPRESENTATIVE: Some hotels have a United States representative through whom reservations can be made. Many of these representatives have a toll free telephone number for your convenience. This is an extremely convenient and efficient way to secure a reservation. However you might find it less expensive to make the reservation yourself since sometimes a representative makes a charge for his service, reserves only the more expensive rooms, or quotes a higher price to protect himself against currency fluctuations and administrative costs. Furthermore, usually only the larger or more expensive hotels can afford the luxury of a representative in the United States. Nevertheless, if you understand that it might cost you more, contacting the hotel representative is an easy way to make a reservation. If a hotel has a representative, it is listed in the back of the book, along with the telephone number, under the specific hotel's description.

INFORMATION

If you have questions not answered in this guide or need special guidance for a particular destination, the Italian Government Travel Offices can assist you. Note: These offices are usually open only from 9am-1pm, Monday through Friday.

Italian Government Travel Office, telephone: (212) 245-4822
630 Fifth Avenue, Suite 1565, New York, NY 10111

Italian Government Travel Office, telephone: (415) 392-6206
360 Post Street, Suite 801, San Francisco, CA 94108

Italian Government Travel Office, telephone: (312) 644-0990
500 North Michigan Avenue, Suite 1046, Chicago, IL 60611

Italian Government Travel Office, telephone: (514) 866-7667
3 Place Ville Marie, Montreal, Quebec, Canada

ITINERARIES

In the first section of this guide you should be able to find an itinerary, or section of an itinerary, that can be easily custom tailored to fit your exact time frame and suit your own particular interests. If your time is limited, you could certainly follow just a segment of an itinerary. In the itineraries we have not specified number of nights at each destination, since to do so seemed much too confining. Again, personality dictates what is best for a particular situation. Some travellers like to see as much as possible in a short period of time and do not mind rising with the birds each morning to begin a new adventure. For others, just the thought of packing and unpacking each night makes them shudder in horror and they would never stop for less than three or four nights at any one destination. A third type of tourist doesn't like to travel at all: the destination is the focus and he will use this guide to find the "perfect" resort from which he will never wander except for daytime excursions. So, once again, use this guide as a reference from which to plan your very own personalized trip.

Please note that although a hotel is suggested for each destination in an itinerary, the hotel is just that - a *SUGGESTION*. Perhaps the hotel seems over your budget, or too fancy, or too simple. Or just not "you". If this is the case just look in the back of the book and choose an alternative.

MAPS

With each itinerary there is a map showing the routing and suggesting places of interest along the way. These are artist's renderings and are not intended to replace a good commercial map. To supplement our generalized routings you will need a set of detailed maps which will indicate all of the highway numbers, expressways, alternate little roads, expressway access points, exact mileages, etc. Our suggestion is to purchase a comprehensive selection of both city maps and regional maps before your departure, and with a highlight pen mark your own "personalized" itinerary and pinpoint your city hotels. If you live in a metropolitan area you should have no problem buying maps in a travel bookstore or else your local bookstore should be able to place a special order. Our personal preference for Italy are the Rand McNally *HALLWAG* maps (there are Rand McNally stores in most major cities simplifying their purchase). Depending upon your itinerary, you need either their map of "Southern Italy" or "Northern Italy" or both (the map that covers the whole of Italy is too general). Each comes with a small index booklet to help you find the towns you are seeking. Almost every town in our guide can be found on the Hallwag maps. Quite frankly, finding some of the small inns we recommend is sometimes really a problem: to help you get at least "warm" as to where the inn of your choice is hiding, in each hotel description we give the kilometers to a well-known city and also to the nearest town that shows on most maps. On pages 97-111 are various regional maps which help you find hotel choices in the area where you are looking for places to stay.

SECURITY WHILE TRAVELLING

The Italians make wonderful hosts. They are friendly, outgoing, gregarious and merry - no one is a "stranger". In fact, it seems every Italian has a brother or cousin in the United States, and so the warmth of camaraderie is further enhanced. In spite of the overall graciousness of the Italians, there are a few "misfits" who have instilled in some tourists the idea that theft is rampant in Italy. True, there are stories about cars being pilfered and purses snatched, but this happens all over the world. Just be cautious. Watch your purse. Don't let your wallet stand out like a red light in your back pocket. Lock your valuables in the hotel vault. Use travelers' checks. Don't leave valuables temptingly exposed in your car. In other words, use common sense. Unfortunately, we have heard of incidents of a group of gypsy children who flock to you, usually in congested, tourist areas, and attempt to steal your wallet or purse. If this should happen to you, shoo them away and call for the police. Note: whenever you travel to any country, it is wise to make a photocopy of the pages of your passport showing your picture, passport number, where issued, etc. With this in hand, in case you lose your passport, it is much easier to get a replacement.

SHOPPING

Italy is a shopper's paradise. Not only are the stores brimming with tempting merchandise, but their displays are beautiful, from the tiniest fruit market to the most chic boutique. Each area has its "specialty". In Venice items made from blown glass and handmade lace are very popular. Milan is famous for its clothing and silkwear (gorgeous scarves, ties and blouses). Florence is a paradise for leather goods (purses, shoes, wallets, gloves, suitcases) and also for gold jewelry (you can buy gold jewelry by weight).   Rome is a fashion center where you can stroll the pedestrian shopping streets browsing in some of the world's most elegant, sophisticated shops where you can buy the latest designer creations and, of course, religious items are available, especially near St Peter's Cathedral.   Naples and the surrounding regions (Capri, Ravello, Positano) offer delightful coral jewelry and also a wonderful selection of ceramics.

TRANSPORTATION

TRAINS: Italy has an excellent network of trains.   The major express trains are usually a quick, reliable way to whip between the major cities.   In contrast, the local trains stop at every little town, take much longer, and are frequently delayed. Each train station is well organized.   There is almost always an information desk where someone who speaks English who will answer any questions and advise you as to the best schedules.   There is another counter where you purchase your tickets.   Still a third counter is where seat reservations are made.   If you can possibly plan ahead, I strongly recommend purchasing your train tickets in advance since it quite time consuming to stand in two lines at each train station, only to find - particularly in summer - that the train you want is already sold out.   You can purchase open tickets in the United States; however, recently it has become almost impossible to purchase in advance your seat reservations.   When this is the case, go ahead and buy the open tickets and then you can either purchase your seat reservations locally, or else pay the concierge at your hotel to handle this transaction for you.   Note: seat reservations *cannot* be made just before getting on the train - it is best to make them as far in advance as possible.

The very popular Eurail Pass is valid in Italy.   This is a pass which allows unlimited travel on most trains throughout Europe.   However, if you are going to travel only in Italy, then you might want to purchase instead one of the Italian Rail passes which are issued for either 8, 15, 21, or 30 days.   You can choose either first or second class passes.   These passes can be purchased through your travel agent or through the Italian State Railways in New York.

Another note on trains - in the summer when rail traffic is very heavy, unless you make dining car reservations in advance you might not be able to have the fun of eating your meal en route.   If you have not made these reservations, as soon as you board the train, zip down to the dining car and ask to reserve a table.

BOATS: Italy has gorgeous islands dotting her shorelines, a glorious string of lakes gracing her mountains to the north, and romantic canals in Venice.   Luckily Italy's boat system is excellent - enabling the tourist maximum enjoyment of some of Italy's most stunning destinations.   All of Italy's islands are linked to the mainland and serviced frequently by a wonderful maritime network.   The many outlying islands often have overnight ferries which even offer sleeping accommodations and facilities for cars.   The closer islands usually have a choice of conveyances - the hydrofoil which zips quickly across the water or the regular ferry.

One of the highlights of traveling in Italy is to explore her wondrous lakes by hopping on one of the ferry boats which glide romantically between the little villages clustered along the shoreline.   Again, there is usually a choice of either the hydrofoil which darts between the hamlets, or the ferry which glides leisurely across the water and usually offers beverage and food service on board.   The boat schedules are posted at each pier, or you can request a timetable from the Italian

Introduction

tourist office.   One note: these little boats are punctual, to the minute, so be right at the pier with your ticket in hand so you can jump on board during the brief interlude that the boat huddles at the shore.   If at all possible, squeeze in a short boat excursion while in Italy.   It is a treat you will long remember.

WEATHER

Italy is blessed with lovely weather.   However, unless you are a ski enthusiast following the promise of what the majestic mountains have to offer in the winter, or must travel in summer due to school holidays, I highly recommend travelling in spring or fall.   Travel at either of these times has two dramatic advantages: you miss the rush of the summer tourist season when all of Italy is packed, and you are most likely to have beautiful weather.   In spring the meadows are painted with wildflowers and in fall the forests are a riot of color as the trees ready for winter.

Summer can be very hot, especially in the cities, and many hotels are not air conditioned. When they are, an additional charge is frequently included on the bill.

WHAT TO WEAR

During the day informal wear is most appropriate including comfortable slacks for women.   In the evening, if you are at a sidewalk cafe or a simple pizzeria, women do not need to dress up nor men to wear coats and ties.   However, Italy does have some elegant restaurants, where definitely a dress and coat and tie are the proper wear.   I think a basic principle is to dress as you would in any city at home.   There are perhaps a few special situations: the churches are still very conservative and shorts are definitely inappropriate.   In fact, some of the cathedrals still insist that women have their arms covered.   It is rare that a scarf on the head is required, but to wear one is a respectful gesture.

The "layered" effect is ideal for Italy.   Because Italy's climate runs the gamut from always cool in the mountains to frequently very hot in the south, the most efficient wardrobe is one where light blouses and shirts can be "reinforced" by layers of sweaters which can be added or peeled off as the day demands.

Italian Highlights by Train & Boat

Riva
Lake Garda
MILANO
SIRMIONE
Desenzano
VERONA
Padua
VENICE
FLORENCE
ROME
Naples
Pompeii
CAPRI
SORRENTO

⊙ OVERNIGHT STOPS

Italian Highlights by Train & Boat

This itinerary can be journeyed easily by car; however, just the thought of taking an automobile onto an Italian expressway intimidates some of the bravest breed of tourist.   It is true that the Italians love cars and enjoy driving fast: it would seem that many are practicing for the Grand Prix.   But an aversion to driving does not mean that your only alternative is a "package" tour.   Italy can be seen splendidly by train and boat.   This is a glorious way to travel and has many advantages: everyone can watch the scenery instead of the road, a bottle of wine can be savored with lunch, and you all arrive rested and ready to enjoy the sights.   But maybe the best advantage of all is that while using public transportation you will make friends. Perhaps there will be just a smile at first, then maybe the sharing of a piece of fruit, and, later, the admiration of each other's family photographs.   Somehow barriers break down on a long journey and the universal warmth of friendliness - at which the Italians are masters - spans any language barriers.

This itinerary covers some of the most famous destinations within Italy. For a short holiday it is impossible to include all the places of interest, but following this pathway will easily provide you with a glimpse of some of the highlights of Italy and will hopefully tempt you to return quickly to delve more deeply into the wonders that Italy has to offer. This itinerary is woven around towns that are conveniently linked by public transportation. Of course, if your time is extremely limited, this itinerary lends itself well to segmentation. If you cannot travel with us all the way, then choose what fits into your schedule and what most appeals to you. No matter what portion you include, you will be treated to a delightful holiday.

In the following itinerary approximate train and boat times have been included. Please note that these are given only as a reference to show you how the pieces of this itinerary tie together. *Schedules are constantly changing, so these must be verified.* Also, many boats and some trains are seasonal, so be very meticulous in making your plans.

ORIGINATING CITY   MILAN

This highlight tour begins in MILAN, a most convenient city since it is the hub of airline flights from throughout Europe, plus it is blessed with non-stop air service from the United States. Also, Milan is strategically located for trains arriving from all over Europe. Into her busy station trains come rushing via the Gotthard, Simplon and Bernina passes. However, it is not location alone which makes Milan an ideal starting point. Although frequently bypassed as an enormous industrial city, Milan has, at its core, a truly charming metropolis which incorporates delights to please all tastes: some of the best shopping in Italy gorgeously displayed in glass-domed arcades, superb medieval squares snuggled unexpectedly within her boundaries, dazzling cathedrals, fascinating museums, gourmet restaurants, and, of course, La Scala - one of the world's most famous opera houses.

12:00 noon depart Milan by train
 1:12 pm   arrive Desenzano

NOTE: This train usually departs from the Milan Central station, but sometimes the trains depart instead from the Porto Garibaldi station, so it is vital that schedules be checked very carefully.

When the train arrives in the ancient port of Desenzano, you can take a cab to the pier where the hydrofoils, steamers and buses leave for Sirmione. However, although more expensive, taking a cab directly to Sirmione (only about 10 kilometers away) is a splurge but also it is really the most convenient means of transportation since you can be taken directly to your hotel.

SIRMIONE is a walled medieval village fabulously located on a tiny peninsula jutting out into Lake Garda - actually almost an island because you first drive along a narrow thread of land and then magically enter Sirmione across the moat through medieval gates.   Unless you are one of the lucky ones with a hotel for the night, you will not be allowed to pass within the town walls by car since pedestrians only are allowed through the entrance.   But with hotel reservations, you can stop at the information office near the entrance and be given a pass to enter with your car.

There are several hotels in the heart of Sirmione but the most glamorous choice, the VILLA CORTINE PALACE HOTEL, is located in a park-like estate on the outskirts of town.   The entrance is absolutely "Hollywood".   You must ring a bell at the impressive gates which then slowly swing open, allowing you to wind your way up through the truly beautiful park to the hotel which crowns the small hill. Previously, this was a sumptuous private villa.   Now a new wing has been built which doubles the original size.   Although the newer wing looks a bit sterile from the outside, the rooms are delightful and most have better views than those in the old section. Demi-pension (breakfast and dinner) are required if you are staying at the Villa Cortine Palace. In addition, reservations are usually taken only for stays of at least three nights. But neither should prove a problem - you will never want to leave such a romantic setting.

Villa Cortine Palace
Sirmione

From the Villa Cortine Palace Hotel you can easily walk to the wharf in the middle of town and study the boat schedule in order to make the decision of which boat you want to take for your day's excursion. You can either glide around the lake all day and have a snack on board, or you can get off in some small jewel of a town and enjoy lunch at a lakefront cafe. Near your hotel there is also a small train, similar to those we have in some of our parks, which shuttles back and forth to the tip of the Sirmione peninsula, so that those who prefer riding to walking can visit the small church and the Roman ruins.

There are trains almost every hour that cover the half-hour journey between Desenzano and Verona. But if it is a beautiful day it might be much more fun to incorporate some sightseeing into your transportation and take a boat and bus instead. If so, the following gives an idea of how this can be done.

9:50 am depart Sirmione by ferry
1:25 pm arrive Riva

You can have lunch on board the ferry or else you can wait until you reach the medieval town of RIVA, located on the northern shore of Lake Garda. The terrace overlooking the lake at the Hotel Sole, located just across from where the ferry docks, provides a serene luncheon setting. The ancient core of Riva is very small, so it will not take long to stroll the old city before you take one of the buses. These leave fifteen times a day in summer for the ride along the eastern shore of the lake and then go on to Verona.

When you arrive in VERONA you will be delighted. This is a town all too frequently bypassed, but what a prize. The city is filled with medieval charm and proudly boasts one of the most marvelous Roman amphitheaters in Italy. Luckily, Verona has several good hotels to complement her marvelous sights. A delightful choice is the HOTEL DUE TORRI. It is strategically situated for walking, yet offers much more than just location. One of the fun and unique attributes of the hotel is the decor of its bedrooms: they all vary, each is individually decorated with its own personality and own period of furniture. If the hotel is not full, there is a clever slide presentation in the lobby which allows you to choose from its picture the bedroom which most suits your fancy. Even if your particular favorite bedroom is not available, you will still enjoy quality accommodation, as all the rooms feature genuine antique furnishings, usually quite ornate and elegant, mostly from the 19th Century.

Hotel due Torri
Verona

DESTINATION III   VENICE

When you are ready to leave Verona, there is frequent train service to Venice so the following is just a suggestion.

2:20 pm depart Verona by train
3:50 pm arrive Venice, Santa Lucia station

As you come out of the front door of the train station you will find that the station is directly on the Grand Canal and that it is a few short steps down to where you can board a boat to take you to your hotel.   The Vaporetto is the most popular means of transportation and is very inexpensive.   This is like a "boat bus" which constantly shuttles back and forth from the train station to St Mark's Square.   The Number Two ferry makes only major stops while the Number One ferry pauses at every stop to exchange passengers.   Much more expensive, but a little faster, is the Motoscafo which is like a water-taxi and will take you wherever you want to go provided there is a motor boat dock. The Gondolas are much slower and even more expensive thus you should probably save your gondola ride for a romantic interlude rather than a train connection.

VENICE has many hotels in every price range. If you want to splurge, stay at the very expensive, very deluxe, GRITTI PALACE, a former home of the immensely wealthy Doge Andrea Gritti. It is easy to imagine the grandeur of days gone by as you arrive in style at the hotel's dock on the Grand Canal and descend onto the red carpet, past the diners enjoying a snack on the deck, and into the beautiful lobby. If money is no object, go all the way and request a room overlooking the canal. Note: in the hotel description section, many more reasonably priced hotels are suggested.

Hotel Gritti Palace
Venice

Venice has so many sights: marvelous restaurants, beautiful boutiques, and fascinating little alleyways to explore, that you could happily stay for weeks. Of course, you will want to savor all the ambiance of St Mark's Square and visit the Doges' Palace. See the Clock Tower whose huge bronze figures bang out the hours with massive hammers. Wander through the museums. Go either on your own or on a tour to the three islands: MURANO (famous for its hand-blown glass), BURANO (famous for its colorfully painted fishermen's cottages and the making of lace), and TORCELLO (once an important city but now just a small village with only its lovely large church to remind one of its past glories). A real bargain is to board the Vaporetto and enjoy the many wonderful palaces bordering the Grand Canal. A favorite pastime in Venice is wandering - just anywhere - exploring the maze of twisting canals and criss-crossing back and forth over some of the 400 toy-like bridges.

Another outing you will certainly enjoy is to take the Il Burchiello, named for a famous 17th-century Venetian boat, which leaves Tuesdays, Thursdays and Saturdays at about 9:20 am from Pontile Giarinetti pier at St Mark's Square and travels the network of rivers and canals linking Venice and Padua. (The schedule might change, so verify.) This little boat, with an English speaking guide on board, stops at several of the exquisite palaces en route. Lunch is served and there is time for sightseeing in Padua before returning to Venice by bus. It is a delightful excursion.

DESTINATION IV   FLORENCE

There are several direct trains each day from Venice to Florence: however, in summer, space is at a real premium, so be sure to reserve a seat in advance. Some of the express trains must have prior seat reservations and will require a supplemental fee. NOTE: During the busy season, if you want to dine on the train it is necessary to make advance reservations when you buy your ticket.

12:00 noon depart Venice, Santa Lucia station (train "Marco Polo")
 3:08 pm   arrive Florence

In FLORENCE, a very good choice for accommodation is the LUNGARNO HOTEL, which rises directly from the banks of the Arno very near the Ponte Vecchio. The Lungarno is not an "old-world" hotel, but rather a modern, very tastefully decorated, charming hotel perched directly on the Arno only a few steps from the heart of Florence. Although new, the Lungarno happily qualifies without too much stretch of the imagination for this guide because it incorporates into its construction a 13th-century tower in which there are some romantic rooms. However, our preference would be a room in the front overlooking the river - a few even have balconies for those lucky travellers who book well in advance.

Lungarno Hotel
Florence

Be generous with your time and do not rush Florence - there is too much to see. You must, of course, pay a visit to Michelangelo's David in the Accademia (located just off the Piazza San Marco), and you must not miss the fantastic museums and cathedrals - the world will probably never again see a city which has produced so much artistic genius. Travellers best appreciate Florence when they are simply roaming. Wander through the streets and poke into small boutiques. Stop in churches which catch your eye - they all abound with masterpieces. Sit to enjoy a cappuccino in one of the little sidewalk cafes and "people watch". Stroll through the piazzas and watch some of the artists at work - many of them incredibly clever - as they paint portraits and do sculptures for a small fee. End your day by finding the perfect small restaurant for delicious pasta made by mama in the back kitchen.

DESTINATION V   ROME

There is excellent train service from Florence to Rome. It is probably best to take one of the midday trains which will allow you to enjoy lunch as you soak in the beauty of the Tuscany hills flowing by your window. Remember that you will need both seat and dining reservations.

11:41 am depart Florence via train
1:48 pm arrive Rome, Termini station

As the train pulls into ROME, you might feel overwhelmed by its size and confusion of traffic, but once you settle into the inviting HOTEL D'INGHILTERRA, surrounded by a maze of captivating shopping streets, you will realize that Rome is not so uncontrollable after all. Many sights in the old city are right at your front door, just waiting to be explored - and Rome is a wonderful city for walking.

Rome is bursting with a wealth of fantastic museums, ancient monuments, spectacular cathedrals, gourmet restaurants, beautiful boutiques, colorful piazzas, whimsical fountains, inspiring statues, theater, opera ... the city itself is virtually a museum. One cannot possibly savor it all. Do get an excellent guidebook and decide what is top priority for your own special interests. If there are several in your party, then a private guide might be money well spent since he will custom tailor your sightseeing. With a private guide you can squeeze much more quality sightseeing into a short period of time.

Hotel d'Inghilterra
Rome

DESTINATION VI   SORRENTO

One could spend weeks discovering the museum that is Rome, but if you have time to add a few more highlights before your return, try to include Sorrento and Capri. There is frequent train service from Rome to Naples and from there it is a short Aliscafi (hydrofoil) ride to Capri. However, for the adventurous it is fun to include Pompeii and Sorrento en route. Please be advised that this makes a long day of travel and takes some manipulating of schedules, but the rewards are great.

You will need an early start to accomplish a tour of Pompeii on your way to Sorrento, but this is a must. How could you be so close without visiting this intriguing city of the Romans which was destroyed, yet preserved forever by the ashes of Vesuvius?

9:00 am depart Rome, Termini station
11:44 am arrive Pompeii, Main station

You *arrive* in POMPEII at the Main station, but you will *depart* from Pompeii at the Villa d. Misteri station, located just across from the main entrance to the archaeological site. Since you will need to store your baggage while you sightsee, take a cab from the Main station to the Villa d. Misteri station and check your suitcases, then you can just walk across the street to the main gate of Pompeii. There is a nice terrace restaurant by the entrance and also a cafe inside. If you want to do your own touring, you can buy a guidebook in English from a stall, or else you can negotiate with one of the licensed guides for a personal tour. You may have heard that the earthquake of 1980 destroyed much of Pompeii. It is true that many of the sites were damaged and some are still under reconstruction, but do not worry, there is still enough to keep you busy for hours. An aura of mystery lingers in the air as you wander the streets of Pompeii. All visitors are touched by this ancient city which, in one day, became frozen for all time.

As you explore Pompeii, there is no need to watch your clock because there is a fun, narrow gauge train departing from the Pompeii Villa d. Misteri station about every twenty minutes for the half-hour scenic journey to Sorrento.

When you arrive in SORRENTO, stay at the GRAND HOTEL EXCELSIOR VITTORIA, a romantic old villa at the center of town in a prime cliff location overlooking the harbor. The hotel's once perfect grandeur is perhaps a bit faded, but as you sit on the terrace in the evening and watch the sun turning the bay to shades of red and gold, the atmosphere is perfection. There is also a pool for relaxing and sunning. Definitely ask for a deluxe room with a view.

Grand Hotel Excelsior Vittoria
Sorrento

DESTINATION VII   CAPRI

When it is time to leave Sorrento there is excellent service by either hydrofoil or ferry to Capri. Perhaps the following schedule will give you a suggestion:

5:45 pm depart Sorrento by hydrofoil
6:30 pm arrive Capri

Your hydrofoil will arrive at the Marina Grande where you will find major hotel representatives on the pier. They will relieve you of your luggage and take it directly to your room in the hotel of your choice, freeing you to take either a mini-bus or the funicular to the main town of CAPRI.

There are many small hotels on Capri but, if you want to splurge, a deluxe hotel choice is the GRAND HOTEL QUISISANA. A larger hotel than most recommended in this guide, it is an oasis at the heart of Capri where you can escape the heat of the day and relax by the beautiful pool. During the day, the island is swarming with tourists who come on day tours. You might surmise that in the evening the activity subsides; but it isn't so. The tour groups leave at dusk but then a new group of people emerge from the deluxe villas and fancy hotels: guests in chic clothes and fancy jewelry strolling the streets - both to see and be seen.

Grand Hotel Quisisana
Capri

Capri has many wonders. The most famous is its submerged cave, the BLUE GROTTO, which can be reached by boat when the seas are calm. Large boats begin leaving the harbor every morning at 9:00 am for the short ride to the entrance to the Blue Grotto, where you are transferred into tiny rowboats. The excursion is an adventure in itself. As your little boat approaches the tiny cave opening it seems impossible that there will be adequate room, but suddenly the sea surges forward and in you squeeze.   Like magic you see it - the mysterious stunning blue light reflecting from some hidden source which illuminates the grotto.

Capri is also a marvelous island for walking. As you stroll the trails, all your senses will be treated by the fragrant flowers, the gorgeous vistas of the brilliant blue waters and the sound of birds luring you ever onward. There are many spectacular walks.   Follow the trail winding down the cliffs to the small harbor on the opposite side called MARINA PICCOLA.   There are lovely views of the shimmering aqua waters as you make your way to the small beach where you can enjoy a swim before your return.   Instead of walking back up the hill, take the little bus which will deliver you quickly back to the main square.

Another absolutely spectacular walk - although a long one of at least 45 minutes each way - is to EMPEROR TIBERIUS'S PALACE, perched high on the cliffs on the western tip of the island.   The panoramic views are stunning.   You have an overview of the whole island and watch the ferries shuttling back and forth to the mainland.   This spot among the ruins makes the perfect picnic spot, so pack a feast of famous Italian salami, cold pasta salad and fruity Soave wine, and soak in the view.

A much shorter walk, but one equally as beautiful, is to the Cannone Belvedere. This path guides you near delightful private villas hidden behind high walls (you can get glimpses through the gates) and on to a promontory overlooking the sea.

When the real world calls and you must leave Capri, there is frequent ferry or hydrofoil service back to Naples.   From there, you can take either a train to Rome or a plane to your next destination.

Mountain &
Lake Adventures

● **OVERNIGHT STOPS**

Mountain & Lake Adventures

For the traveller who wants to combine the magic of seeing some of the world's most splendid mountains with the joy of visiting Italy's scenic northern lakes, this itinerary will be ideal. Contrasts will heighten the impact of visual delights as you meander through lovely mountain passes, via lush green meadows laced with wildflowers, beneath giant mountains piercing the sky with their jagged granite peaks, and bordering lazy blue lakes whose steep shorelines are decorated with endearing little Italian villages wrapped in misty cloaks of wonderful siennas and ochers. What a glorious holiday to wind across northern Italy enjoying some of its most beautiful landscapes. This itinerary can stand alone. However, it is also perfect for the traveller arriving or departing from neighboring countries. We have carefully shown detours for the tourist who will be leaving or entering from Austria, Switzerland, or France. All too often the tourist thinks he has "finished" Italy when his tour ends in Venice and he too quickly rushes north into Austria or Switzerland. What a waste. A very promising picturesque region still remains. Please try to linger to enjoy some of the mountains and lakes which truly are some of Italy's greatest natural treasures.

ORIGINATING CITY   VENICE

This itinerary begins in VENICE, one of the most romantic cities in the world. Her many narrow waterways are criss-crossed by storybook bridges and shadowed by majestic palaces whose soft hues reflect warmly in the shimmering water. Black gondolas quietly glide through the narrow canals as the gondolier in his red and white striped shirt softly serenades his romantic passengers with an operatic selection. Venice is not a traditional city, rather an archipelago of 117 islands "glued" together by 400 bridges.

DESTINATION I   ASOLO

You need not rush your departure this morning. Venice is a city that should be enjoyed slowly and since your journey today is short, you can certainly have the luxury of a last leisurely breakfast before embarking on your next adventure.

Since all the "streets" in Venice are liquid, you will need to take a boat to your car. It will probably be at the Piazzale Roma where most of the car rental companies are located: in addition it is also where there are overnight car parks for storing your car if you drive into Venice. The choice of conveyance will depend upon your budget and your inclination. The Vaporetto is the most reasonable. Similar to a river bus, the Vaporetto leaves regularly from St Mark's Square for the approximately half-hour ride to the Piazzale Roma. The Vaporetto Number One stops at most of the little docks along the route whereas Vaporetto Number Two is an express boat which stops at only a few major points. The Motoscafi are motorboats which duck through the back canals and usually take about fifteen minutes to the Piazzale Roma. The Motoscafi are like private cabs and are much more expensive than the "bus", but can be very convenient, especially if your hotel has a private motor boat landing.   The most deluxe mode of transportation is by private Gondola: however, these are very expensive and usually take about an hour to reach the Piazzale Roma.

Once you have retrieved your car from the parking garage or have finished the paper work for your car rental, head north from Venice toward TREVISO which requires about an hour's drive.   If time allows, stop here.   Stroll through this picturesque city spider-webbed with canals and surrounded by 15th-century ramparts.   Perhaps have a cup of coffee or a bite of lunch before heading north toward Asolo.   Treviso is famous for its arcaded streets, churches lavishly decorated with frescos, and many delightfully painted houses.   You might want to climb the ramparts for a view of the Alps beckoning you on.   From Treviso it is approximately another hour to Asolo.   However, just a few miles before you reach Asolo you should see signs for the town of MASER where the marvelous VILLA DI MASER (some of your books might use the name of VILLA BARARO) is located. This is a splendid villa designed by Palladio and fabulously decorated with frescos by Paolo Veronese.   This elegant villa has erratic days and hours when it is open to the public - usually in late afternoons on Tuesdays, Saturdays and Sundays. However, it is only about one mile out of your way, so well worth a detour to investigate.   There is also a very interesting museum of old carriages and antique cars at Villa di Maser.

Your prize tonight is ASOLO.   It is an absolute delight, a gem of a medieval village snuggled on the side of a hill with exquisite views of the countryside.   As you drive toward Asolo the terrain does not seem to hold much promise - just modern towns and industry - but then the road winds up a lovely hillside and into the tiny village which encompasses a delightful combination of a "real" town of colorful fruit stands, candy shops, and the neighborhood grocer for those lucky few who live in Asolo; plus, gorgeous shops with exquisite merchandise for the tourist. Of course a castle adorns the hill above the village - mostly in ruins but setting the proper stage.   Naturally, there is a wonderful cathedral dominating the square, just as it should.   You will find all this plus vineyards and olive trees on the hillsides and the scent of roses in the air. No wonder Robert Browning fell in love with Asolo and chose it as his home. It might not be possible for all to live here, but at least you have the marvelous option of staying at the VILLA CIPRIANI, a superb villa. In this lovely hotel which was once the home of Robert Browning, you too can pretend that Asolo is yours as you sit on the peaceful terrace and watch the soft lights paint the distant villa-dotted hills in mellow shades of gold.

Hotel Villa Cipriani
Asolo

DESTINATION II   CORTINA

There are a couple of towns which are worth seeing before leaving the Asolo area. If brandy holds a special interest for you, visit BASSANO DEL GRAPPA, an old town famous for its production of grappa (or brandy). The town is also a pottery center. However, it is rather large, and, in my estimation, much less interesting than a tiny town just a few miles farther on, MAROSTICA. If you are in this area in September, check your calendar and consider a stop in Marostica because during the first part of September - in alternate years - the central square is transformed into a giant chess board and local citizens become the human chess pieces. Even if it isn't the year of the chess game, Marostica is a picturesque little medieval town encircled by ramparts whose pretty central square is formed by colorful buildings and castle walls. There is also a second castle guarding the town from the top of the hill.

As you head north into the Dolomites there are various routes from which to choose. The major highway heads north through Feltre and Belluno and then on to Cortina. However, if the day is nice and your spirit of adventure is high, there is really nothing more fun than the "back roads" through the mountains. Journey through tiny hamlets and gorgeous mountain valleys far from the normal tourist path; always keeping a map somewhere accessible so that you don't wind up hopelessly lost.

You might want to travel casually and choose your own little country inn in one of the lovely little valleys of the Dolomites, but if you are making reservations, a good choice for an overnight stop is CORTINA D'AMPEZZO. This is not a small town. In fact, it has grown into a large tourist center due to its excellent skiing facilities: however, the location is truly superb, with gigantic granite peaks ringing the town. In Cortina there are many hotels. One with a history that dates back far before the skiing craze is the MENARDI. According to the Menardi family, this was originally a peasant farm house located along one of the main mountain passes. Because so many travellers stopped seeking shelter for the night - more often than not in the hay loft - the house gradually became an inn. Times have changed. Today the Menardi is a proper hotel where the guests sleep in comfortable beds with fine linens and down comforters, and all the bedrooms have private baths. However, much of the original atmosphere remains, with beautiful country antiques cleverly incorporated into the decor. Great taste and personal warmth are felt throughout.

Hotel Menardi
Cortina

Although the Menardi was originally a farmhouse, civilization has crept in and today the inn is located on the north side of Cortina directly on the main highway heading toward Toblach.

DESTINATION III   VAL D'EGA - OBEREGGEN

When it is time to leave Cortina for further mountain adventures you will be taking the Old Dolomite Road heading west from Cortina to Bolzano. This historic pass was originally used by the merchants of Venice on their way to Germany. Follow the highway S48 from Cortina which will take you over a windswept barren pass surrounded by towering granite peaks. The road then drops into a valley before climbing again to conquer the Pordoi Pass and then down into the Fassa Valley.

When you reach the town of Vigo di Fassa leave the road you are on and head west over the Carezza Pass. Along the way on your left you will pass Lake Carezza which, although small, is certainly worth a stop as it is an enchanting green lake surrounded by mountain peaks. Soon after leaving Lake Carezza you arrive in the town of Nova Levante.

The route from Cortina to Nova Levante is well marked, but from this town on you will need to watch for the road signs. Just a few miles beyond Nova Levante you will come to a junction. At this intersection take the road to the left and, keeping to the left, follow the signs for EGA, EGGEN, OBEREGGEN, or SAN FLORIANO. In this part of Italy the town names are most confusing because each town is named both in Italian and also with its old Austrian name (before the first World War this section of Italy belonged to the Austrian Empire). So, Ega and Eggen are the same town, and Obereggen and San Floriano are the same town.

Hotel Bewallerhof
Val d'Ega, Obereggen

After leaving Nova Levante, the HOTEL BEWALLERHOF is located between Ega and Obereggen. If it sounds complicated to find, it is. You will probably get lost along the way, but just stop and ask directions and make certain you have a detailed map. (The best ones, which you will be able to find in Cortina, are the VERY detailed hiking path maps which also have the highways indicated.) If the weather is clear this route from Cortina to Obereggen will take you through some of the most breath-taking mountains on earth.

Whereas your last hotel was in the bustling town of Cortina, the Bewallerhof is almost as isolated as a hotel can be. Leaving the town of Ega (or Eggen) you will soon see a sign on the side of the road reading "Bewallerhof". Turn here and you will weave through a pine forest which then opens into a meadow graced by a small hotel, built upon the site of an old farmhouse (this is still farming country with pastures and cows nearby adding to the country ambiance). The deck dominating the front of the hotel has a panoramic view which stretches for miles over grassy fields which sweep across to rows of mountains. Behind the hotel the granite peaks of the Dolomites rise dramatically in the sky forming a majestic natural backdrop.

For some tastes the Bewallerhof will be too isolated. For some personalities the hotel will be too basic. But you will definitely not be "roughing it": all the rooms have private baths and although the decor is simple, it is very inviting with light wooden furniture, plants, and paneling. The emphasis, however, is on the outdoors. What bliss to walk for miles in any direction surrounded by such beauty. Note: an alternate choice of accommodation is the Gasthof Obereggen, located in the nearby village of Obereggen (page 233). This small inn is quite simple, but you will be given a wonderful welcome.

If you are a mountain enthusiast you might just decide to stay forever in the beautiful Val e'Ega, but when it is time to continue on, be consoled by the fact that there is another beautiful mountain region and lovely hotel awaiting at the end of your day's journey, plus an interesting town to visit en route.

When you depart from Obereggen, return to the main road, marked S241, and follow the splendid Val d'Ega (Ega Valley) as it weaves its way through a dramatic gorge.   The road joins the main expressway just north of Bolzano where you take the E6 expressway north to BRESSANONE.   Try to time your stop at Bressanone for lunch because this small city has much to offer: a walled medieval town ringed by mountains, it has a charming little village square plus a river (lined on both banks by promenades) meandering through its center.   Bressanone hides another treasure, the HOTEL ELEFANT.   This inn is famous for its exquisite cuisine.   In its beautiful dining rooms only the freshest foods and wines are served - usually from the hotel's own farms and vineyards.   But the hotel also has an intriguing tale: in the 16th Century an elephant was being delivered to Maximilian of Austria as a special gift.   Well, it seems this "gift" grew weary of walking by the time it arrived in Bressanone and so was housed at the local inn - you guessed it - the Elefant.   The story alone merits a stop, but the joy is that the Elefant also retains so much character and serves such excellent food.

From Bressanone take the expressway north toward the Brenner Pass, soon leaving the expressway near Vipiteno to head southwest along a twisting road which maneuvers along the Monte Giovo Pass as it twists its way through the mountains and then drops down into the valley to follow the Passiria River which winds a path into Merano.

DETOUR NOTE: If your destination is Austria, then at Vipiteno continue north on the expressway for the short drive to the Brenner Pass leading into Austria.

In MERANO the CASTEL FREIBERG is an enchanting fairytale castle which majestically dominates the surrounding countryside from its hillside perch. This fabulous castle has everything - setting, view, marvelous architecture, gourmet food, beautiful rooms, priceless antiques, pool, tennis, and friendly.

Castel Freiberg
Merano

DESTINATION V   SAN VIGILIO

It is a short drive south from Merano to Bolzano where you will meet the freeway heading toward Trent, the town where the Catholic council met in the 16th Century to establish important articles of faith which emphasized the authority of the Catholic church.

Locanda San Vigilio
San Vigilio

Leave the freeway at Trent and head west on 45 toward the small, but lovely, green LAKE TOBLINO which is enhanced by a superb castle on its north shore where you can stop for lunch. From Toblino head south on the pretty country road, lined with fruit trees and vineyards, heading directly south toward Lake Garda, Italy's largest lake. When you come to ARCO, the road splits. Take the road to the left and continue south to Lake Garda and then follow 249 as it curves along the eastern shore of the lake.

About 4 kilometers beyond the town of Torri d Benaco, turn right when you see San Vigilio sign posted. There is a gate where you will be stopped by an attendant who will want you to pay for parking (San Vigilio is also a park). Say you are a guest at the hotel and you will be allowed to pass. Drive as far as you can and then park your car. At the stately villa behind tall gates, turn left and follow the lane until it deadends at the LOCANDA SAN VIGILIO, a 16th-century stone building, so close to the water's edge that waves lap beneath the windows. With such a setting, it is not surprising that Winston Churchill used to come here to paint. Inside, you will not be disappointed. The rooms are tastefully decorated with country antiques complemented by color coordinated fabrics. If you want to splurge, ask for a suite overlooking the lake, but no matter which room you choose, they are all most appealing. There is a romantic dining room where you can eat in your own little niche by a window overlooking the lake.

When you are ready to sightsee, drive a few kilometers further south along the lake to GARDA. Park your car and take one of the ferries or hydrofoils which ply the lake. If you have the time, choose a different destination each day - perhaps planning to have a bite of lunch at an enticing little lakeside cafe. If have time for only one adventure, visit SIRMIONE, a wonderful walled village at the south end of Lake Garda positioned at the end of a miniature peninsula which proudly pokes its head into the lake. During the summer this town is absolutely bursting with tourists, but you can easily understand why: this is another one of Italy's "stage setting" villages, almost too perfect to be true. If you take the ferry or hydrofoil to Sirmione, your boat will dock in the center of the town and you can stroll through the little boutiques, perhaps have a bite of lunch at one of the beautiful terrace cafes overlooking the lake, and explore the tiny island-like village. If you want to go to the tip of the peninsula, there are small motorized trams which you take you there.

If time permits, take the ferry to RIVA on the northern shore of the lake. Although, much of the town is of new construction, the medieval core with its Piazza III Novembre and 13th-century Tower of Apponale is fun to see. A good place to eat lunch on the terrace of the HOTEL SOLE (page 202), located directly across fom the boat dock.

Another excursion is by car to GARDONE RIVIERA (on the western shore of the lake) to see a nearby museum, the VITTORIALE, once the home of Gabriele

D'Annunzio, the celebrated Italian poet. (For those of us who love stories of romance, D'Annunzio is also famous for his love affair with Eleanora Duse.) While there, if you enjoy gourmet food, the pink and white VILLA FIORDALISO, located right on the lake, is a well-known restaurant (page 159). The Villa Fiordaliso also has a tidbit of historical romance - this was once the hide-away of Mussolini and his mistress, Claretta. For a simpler meal, just a few kilometers further north along the lake at Gargnano-Villa, you can enjoy a wonderful seafood lunch on the sun-drenched deck of the Baia d'Oro (page 161).

DESTINATION VI   BELLAGIO

It might be easier to leave the Locanda San Vigilio knowing that another beautiful lakefront hotel,the GRAND HOTEL VILLA SERBELLONI on Lake Como, awaits your arrival. The Villa Serbelloni will be a nice contrast because although both are on the lakefront, the Locanda San Vigilio is small and intimate whereas the Villa Serbelloni is grand and imposing.

On your way from Lake Garda to Lake Como, stop at BERGAMO, about an hour's drive west on the A4. As you approach Bergamo it will not look worth a stop - but it is. The shell of the city is deceiving because it hides a lovely kernel, the CITA ALTA, or high city. The lower part of Bergamo is modern and congested, but the old medieval city snuggled on the top of the hill holds such treasures as the Piazza Vecchia, the Colleoni Chapel, and the Church of St Mary Major. Should you want to time your stop in Bergamo with lunch, there are several excellent restaurants. A suggestion would be at the Agnello d'Oro, a cozy, charming 17th-century inn in the Cita Alta.

From Bergamo it is a short drive on to BELLAGIO, a medieval port located at the tip of a peninsula dividing the lower section of Lake Como into two lakes, Lake

Como on the west and Lake Lecco on the east.   Your hotel, the Grand Hotel Villa Serbelloni, is found behind gates opening onto the main square of Bellagio.   It is a large imposing "old-world" style palace hotel offering everything you could wish for in a lakeside interlude - tennis, swimming pool, boat excursions, private beach, and more.   The Villa Serbelloni is very ornate, still retaining its glory of bygone days. In fact the hotel is almost overwhelming with its soaring, intricately painted ceilings, heavy chandeliers, and fabulous sweeping staircase.   The setting of the Villa Serbelloni is superb and overshadows what might be perceived as the slightly "faded elegance" of the hotel's decor.   Note: for an less expensive hotel, the family-owned and managed Hotel Florence is very nice (page 118).

Villa Serbelloni
Bellagio

Just a few steps from the hotel lies charming, medieval Bellagio where you can meander through the village or walk to the pier for one of the boats which will take you to all corners of the lake.   What a wonderful excursion.   Lake Como is absolutely beautiful - especially the lower eastern branch of the lake called Lake

Lecco where cliffs enclose the shorelines like gorgeous walls and give a fjord-like beauty to the area.   There are numerous romantic steamers which glide in and out of the picturesque, softly hued little hamlets dotting the lake shore.   You can settle onto a steamer equipped with bar and restaurant and from your armchair lazily enjoy the constantly changing, but always intriguing shoreline as the boat maneuvers in and out of the colorful little harbors, past elegant private villas, by postcard-pretty villages.   From Bellagio you can also step on board one of the swift hydrofoils which will whisk you about the lake.   Or, you can put your car right on the ferry to either Cadenabbia on the western shore of Lake Como or Varenna on the eastern shore. With Bellagio as a base there are several sightseeing possibilities.   An excursion to visit the VILLA CARLOTTA, a fairytale-like 18th-century palace - worthy of the Prussian Princess Carlotta for whom it was named - is enjoyable.   You can take the car ferry from Bellagio to Cadenabbia on the western shore.   From there it is just a short drive along the beautiful tree lined Via del Paradiso to the Villa Carlotta which is encircled by its own gorgeous park of terraced gardens.

DESTINATION VII   ISOLA DEI PESCATORI

DETOUR NOTE: Should your plans call for ending your Italian sojourn and heading on into Switzerland this would be an excellent point to begin your journey. Head north along Lake Como and on to Chiavenna where you then turn east for the short drive (only about 10 kilometers) to the Swiss border.   From there it is a lovely drive through the Engadine Valley to St Moritz.

Continuing on toward LAKE MAGGIORE, take advantage of the expressways to make your drive as easy as possible because there is usually heavy traffic in this part of Italy.   It is best to head directly south from Bellagio to pick up the freeway in the direction of Milan.   Keep on the bypass which skirts to the north of Milan and follow the freeway northwest to Lake Maggiore. When you reach the lake continue along the western shore to STRESA. It seems only suitable that for a "Mountain and Lake Adventure" one of your hotels should be located on an island in a lake - so we have chosen for you one of the Borromean Islands, ISOLA DEI PESCATORI (Fisherman's Island), located in Lake Maggiore. This is an enchanting little island with twisting, narrow alley-like streets and colorful fishermen's cottages. As the name implies, this is still an active fishing village. During the tourist season the island teems with people and the streets are lined with rather tacky souvenir shops, but it is hard to dull the charm of this quaint town.

Hotel Verbano
Isola dei Pescatori

This island can be reached by ferry from Stresa, Baveno, or Pallanza, but the most popular of these is Stresa from which there are frequent departures by boat to Isola dei Pescatori. Your hotel, the VERBANO, is definitely not a deluxe hotel. In fact, it would not be suitable for those who enjoy only fancy hotels because this is a small, very basic hotel. The lobby is quite plain. The bedrooms too are very simple. However, if you appreciate all kinds of hotels for the special attributes they have to offer, you will love the Verbano. It has an enchanting terrace with dining tables set overlooking the lake; the bedrooms too have beautiful vistas and some even offer large patios. The food is delicious, and the service of the Zacchera family, who own and manage the Verbano, is warm and gracious.

This tiny archipelago consisting of Isola Bella (Beautiful Island), Isola dei Pescatori (Fisherman's Island), and Isola Madre (Mother Island) are world famous for their dramatic palaces and spectacular, fragrant gardens. How smug you will feel to settle into your room and then enjoy a drink on the lovely terrace while watching the last of the tourists hustle onto the boat for shore, leaving you to enjoy the sunset.

DESTINATION VIII   CHAMPOLUC

DETOUR NOTE: Should your next destination be Zermatt, then it is time to leave Italy by heading north in the direction of Domodossolo. About 16 kilometers beyond Domodossolo you arrive at Iselle where you drive your car piggyback style onto the train and ride in your car as you zigzag through the fabulous Simplon Tunnel and emerge about 20 minutes later in Brig, Switzerland.

From Verbano drive south to the main freeway and head west toward Turin. Before reaching Turin watch for the signs and take the branch of the expressway heading toward Aosta. When you come to Verres, leave the highway and take the small road north to CHAMPOLUC, an hour's drive. The road follows the Evancon River as it cuts its path through the mountains. At first the valley is quite steep and narrow and then opens up into wide meadows lazily stretching out on both sides of the river. In early summer the meadows are truly lovely, blanketed in brilliantly colored wildflowers.

Anna Maria
Champoluc

Just before the road leaves Champoluc you will see a marker for the ANNA MARIA HOTEL. At this sign turn to the right and follow the road for a very short drive up the hill until you see the hotel. It is beautifully located amid the pine trees and has views in every direction of the spectacular mountains. The Anna Maria is a small chalet-style inn owned and managed by Anna Maria. The dining room is cozy and inviting with gay red checked curtains at the windows and rustic Alpine-style carved wooden chairs. The bedrooms, although small, all have private bathrooms and are very appealing with paneled walls and a country flavor.

When it is time to leave Champoluc you have two options if you want to travel into Switzerland. First you must drive back to the main expressway and head west. In about a half hour you will come to Aosta at which point you can leave the expressway for the road leading north to the San Bernardino tunnel and into expressway for the road leading north to the San Bernardino tunnel and into Switzerland's Rhone Valley. Or, by continuing on the expressway west through the village of Courmayeur, you arrive at the Mont Blanc tunnel which delivers you briefly into France, and then on to Geneva within an hour via main highway. Of course, by taking the short drive to Milan you can easily "tie in" with another Italian holiday suggested in this guide.

Romantic Hilltowns of Tuscany & Umbria

FLORENCE

PANZANO IN CHIANTI

Arezzo

San Gimignano   Siena   Cortona

Abbey of Monte   SINALUNGA   ASSISI

Oliveto Maggiore   Perugia   Torgiano

Pienza

Orvieto   Spoleto   Monteluco

Todi

•ROME

◉ OVERNIGHT STOPS

Romantic Hilltowns of Tuscany & Umbria

Nothing could possibly surpass the exquisite beauty of the countryside near Florence in the spring. It is breathtaking. Actually, any time of the year, if you meander into the hilltowns south of Florence, all your senses will be rewarded with the splendors that this enchanting Italian region has to offer. Almost every hillock is crowned with a picture-perfect little walled village. The fields are brilliant with vibrant red poppies. The vineyards lace the fields in all their glory and promise. The olive trees dress the hillsides in a frock of dusky grey-green. Pine forests unexpectedly appear to highlight the landscape. As if this were not enough, this area is a treasure trove of some of the finest small hotels in all the world. And if this is still not sufficient to tempt you away from the normal tourist route, be reminded that the food and wines of Tuscany and Umbria are superb.

So, when you plan your trip to Italy, please allow time to treat yourself to a unique adventure. Save at least a few days to slip away from the cities and into the country. Perhaps you will not have time to follow this entire itinerary, but at least sneak in a few days in this special region of Italy. You will be well rewarded with a wealth of memories which will linger long after you return home.

ORIGINATING CITY   FLORENCE

Your journey begins in FLORENCE. Allow enough time to savor this marvelous city but, if you are reluctant to leave, be consoled. There are many treats in store for you in the delightful hilltowns which surround Florence. Magnificent art is not confined to the city limits of Florence and you will see impressive cathedrals and beautiful works of art throughout the neighboring areas. Yet the real rewards in store for you are not only the masterpieces created by man, but also those of Nature. (See pages 30-31 for sightseeing tips.)

DESTINATION I   ASSISI

The traffic around Florence is difficult, so find the expressway to Rome and follow it until you come to the turnoff for Arezzo, which is located about 10 kilometers east of the highway. You might want to bypass Arezzo. Although it has a rich, medieval history dating back to the Etruscan era, it is a large city and it is not as quaint as some of its smaller neighbors.

If you follow the main road south from Arezzo, you will soon arrive at CORTONA. This is a beautifully situated walled town climbing up a steep hillside covered with olive trees. Stop to enjoy the atmosphere of this medieval town with its crazy little twisting streets, jumble of small squares and colorful buildings. A mighty castle dramatically stands guard over this hillside town.

Leaving Cortona, continue south to Lake Trasimeno and follow the northern shore on to PERUGIA, a large medieval city encompassed by ramparts. An important Umbrian city since Etruscan days, the heart of the old city is the Piazza IV Novembre, a beautiful square with an especially appealing fountain, the Fontana Maggiore, built in the late 13th Century.

It is only a short drive farther south from Perugia to ASSISI. Even if it were not for the lingering memory of the gentle St Francis, this would be a delightful spot for it is one of the most spectacular of all the hilltowns in Umbria. Perhaps there are a few too many souvenir shops, but this is a small price to pay for such a very special place. The town walls begin on the lower slopes of the valley and perfectly enclose the area as it climbs the steep hillside with a climax in an enormous crowning castle. Assisi is a marvelous town for walking: you will need sturdy shoes to wind your way up and down the puzzle of tiny streets. It is great fun. You will come across intriguing little lanes which open into small squares. When you stop to rest, there will be marvelous vistas of the breathtaking Umbrian fields stretching out below. There is the fabulous St Francis' Basilica which includes a monastery with a beautiful arcaded courtyard.

To truly appreciate the beauty of Assisi, it is fun to spend the night and, luckily, there are several good hotel choices. Beautifully situated with one of its walls forming a section of the piazza of the St Francis' Basilica is the HOTEL SUBASIO. This is not a deluxe hotel but it has much to entice the tourist. Perhaps its most impressive attribute is the view from the vine covered dining terrace over the undulating Umbrian fields which seem to glow with a special radiance. Some of the bedrooms, too, have splendid vistas from their balconies. Definitely splurge and request one of the best rooms so you can capture each possible moment of this very beautiful scene.

Hotel Subasio
Assisi

While staying at Assisi, drive one day the short distance to TORGIANO where there is a splendid wine museum. One would never dream that such a tiny town could boast such a stunning museum, but it is not a coincidence. The Lungarotti family owns the vineyards for miles in every direction and, indeed, they must be a very clever and dedicated family for they also own a delightful hotel in the center of town, LE TRE VASELLE. A charming spot for lunch, Le Tre Vaselle has the ambiance of a lovely country manor house. In addition to overseeing the decoration of this exquisite hotel, Signore Lungarotti also furnished the museum with artifacts pertaining to every aspect of the production of wine from the earliest days. The collection is interesting and beautifully displayed, worthy of a detour by anyone interested in wines. (See page 229.)

Get an early start this morning because it is going to be difficult to squeeze in all of the enchanting hilltop towns en route.   Driving south from Assisi you soon come to SPOLETO, an intriguing town.   Not only is this another of the beautifully preserved medieval cities with a dramatic perched site, but it also has an almost unbelievable bridge dating from Roman times.   It spans the deep ravine between Spoleto and the adjoining mountain, and was built over a Roman aqueduct existing in the 14th Century.   This incredible bridge is 755 feet long and 262 feet high.   It is supported by a series of ten Gothic arches and has a fort at the far end as well as a balcony in the center.

Before leaving the vicinity of Spoleto, if you are a St Francis enthusiast, you make the short detour to visit MONTELUCO, where St Francis came to live as a hermit. You will appreciate why he chose Monteluco after you twist to the top of the mountain and enjoy the glorious view of the surrounding hillsides covered with olive trees.

Make a brief stop, as you head west, at TODI, another of the tiny hilltop walled villages about midway between Spoleto and Orvieto.   However, do not linger too long in Todi because the next town, Orvieto, is the real prize.

ORVIETO is spread across the top of a hill which drops down on every side in steep volcanic cliffs.   One wonders how the town could ever have been built.   At Orvieto's center is a glorious duomo dominating a beautiful piazza.   You may think you have seen enough stunning cathedrals, but this one is really special - brilliantly colored in intricate mosaic designs and accentuated by slender spirals stretching gracefully into the sky.

Also of great interest in Orvieto is the visit to another engineering feat, St Patrick's

Well. This well, over 200 feet deep, was hewn out of solid volcanic rock to collect and store water in case of a siege.

After seeing Orvieto, it might be getting late in the day and you will need to head directly north on the A1 to your night's destination, SINALUNGA. But, if you have time, explore the small back roads, winding through the countryside as you head north. As a goal, mark on your Hallwag map the tiny hilltop town of PIENZA as your first target. It does not matter if you get a little lost. The scenery is beautiful and you will make discoveries of your own. An example of unspoiled beauty: Pienza has no modern developments to interrupt its charm. Within its walls, you will find quaint little squares and a church built almost on the edge of the ramparts affording a lovely terrace view. About 36 kilometers north of Pienza is the ABBEY OF MONTE OLIVETO MAGGIORE (also on Hallwag map), serenely situated among the cypress forest. Of special interest are the terra cottas adorning the entrance, created by the famous artist, Luca della Robbia. The cloisters contain frescos portraying the life of St Benedict.

Locanda dell'Amorosa
Sinalunga

From the Abbey, drive east to the town of SINALUNGA where there is a delightful (though quite expensive) hotel, the LOCANDA DELL'AMOROSA. The lane leading to the Locanda dell'Amorosa is lined on both sides with tall cypress trees through which you glimpse an expanse of vineyards. The town walls mark the hotel's entrance, as the hotel is the town. Pass through the gate into a large courtyard (at its end is an exquisite little church). The wing of buildings to the left contains the bedrooms. The wing to the right houses the reception lounge and the attractive dining room which is well-known for its food. In this same little "hotel-town" a delicious wine is bottled which you can sample at dinner.

DESTINATION III   PANZANO IN CHIANTI

On your way to Panzano be sure to stop in SIENA, another of the strategically built walled hilltowns. This is an entrancing city and deserves many hours to savor all its attributes. The ramparts are perfectly preserved with massive gates guarding a meticulously maintained medieval stronghold. Drive as close as you can to the main square and park your car. All sightseeing can and should be done by foot. The giant piazza is a sight in itself: it is immense and, instead of being square, is fan shaped. All the streets surrounding the square end like the spokes of a giant wheel in the Piazza del Campo. The town hall monopolizes one side of the piazza with graceful arches embellished with the coat of arms of Siena. It is in this gigantic piazza that the colorful "Palio delle Contrade" takes place in July and August every year. The horse race is only a part of this colorful spectacle of medieval costumes, wonderful banners and parades. You can check for the exact dates, but the festivities extend beyond the actual date of the races. Also, Siena has one of Italy's most dramatic cathedrals, located a short walk from the Piazza del Campo. Not only is the cathedral striking - with its bold patterns of black and white marble - but it also houses a museum.

From Siena, continue north on the expressway and take the turnoff for SAN GIMIGNANO. Although you might think you are weary of walled towns, San Gimignano is unique and definitely worth a stop. What is so dramatic about San Gimignano is that at one time this small walled village was surrounded by 72 towers. During the Middle Ages it was a status symbol for noble families to each build personal towers for protection: the higher the tower, the greater the image of wealth and importance. It is amazing that fourteen of the original towers of San Gimignano are still standing. They make a striking silhouette soaring like skyscrapers: on a clear day, you can see them on the horizon from miles away. In addition to the romance of the towers, San Gimignano is a charming medieval village and there is an excellent restaurant (also a delightful hotel), LA CISTERNA, found on the main square.

Villa le Barone
Panzano in Chianti

From San Gimignano, head almost directly east to PANZANO IN CHIANTI where the prize of your journey, VILLA LE BARONE, awaits you. This is an exquisite small hotel encompassing all the joys that are Tuscany. This villa was once the home of the Della Robbia family, and today is owned by Duchessa Franca Viviani Della Robbia. The location is idyllic: the villa is set in lovely gardens and surrounded by vineyards. There is a welcoming pool. A terrace for dining overlooks a panorama of the Tuscany hills stretching for miles in the distance while another dining room is fashioned from the former stables. Breakfast and dinner are included in the price of a room and reservations during the high season are usually accepted only for a stay of several days: but this is no problem ... you will want to stay forever.

When it is time to complete your loop and return to Florence you will find it only about an hour's drive away in time but years away in mood from the tranquility of the Villa le Barone.

Rome to Milan
via the Italian Riviera

MILAN

Pavia Carthusian Monastery

Genoa
Camogli
Chiavari
PORTOFINO
Carrara
Cinque Terre
La Spezia
LUCCA
FLORENCE
Pisa

ROME

⊙ OVERNIGHT STOPS

SWITZERLAND

AUSTRIA

FRANCE

67

Rome to Milan via the Italian Riviera

This itinerary includes one of the most picturesque jewels of Italy, the Italian Riviera, where not only are there charming towns snuggled into small coves along the shoreline, but the road itself is a masterpiece of engineering. The coastal highway along the Riviera "bridges" for miles - high in the sky above the ravines - and "tunnels" in and out of the cliffs rising steeply from the sea. The original title for this itinerary was "Coastal Route from Rome to Milan", but after we personally experienced the drive, the route and the name were changed. There is an expressway partially following the coast from Rome to Pisa, but until this is finished the road is one of total frustration with a solid line of trucks and cars making the journey undesirable. Far easier, and actually more scenic, is to take the expressway north from Rome to Florence through the gorgeous Tuscany hills then to head west on to Pisa and finally travel on via the coast to Genoa and Milan. It is impossible to include all of the towns that dot the coastline, but after ducking on and off the freeway ourselves, we have tried to include some of the most charming.

This itinerary begins in ROME, a favorite of all and a wonderful introduction to Italy. In the hotel section of this guide there are many suggestions for accommodations to suit your taste and budget. It would take this entire guide just to give you a taste of what Rome has to offer: the Roman Forum, the Colosseum, St Peter's Basilica, the Vatican, the Spanish Steps, the Arch of Constantine, the Pantheon - these are just a few of the places you must not miss. The whole of Rome is a virtual museum. Buy a paper-back guide book at one of the many bookstores or tourist stands to plan what you want to see and do.

Rome has a rich selection of places to stay: hotels to fit every budget. Browse through the hotel section in the back of this guide for suggestions on hotels. Make a reservation in advance because hotel space is very tight - particularly during the busy tourist season. Plan to stay in Rome for several days at least, then when you are saturated with the overwhelming sights and are ready to continue your journey, buy a detailed city map to assist you in maneuvering out of the city and onto the magnificent expressway heading north.

DESTINATION I   LUCCA

From Rome, take the A1 north toward Florence. This itinerary assumes that you have already visited Florence, certainly one of the highlights of any Italian holiday. If not, you will assuredly want to stop in Florence for several days - there are many wonderful places to stay suggested in the hotel section in the back of this guide. Otherwise, bypass to the south of Florence and take the A11 west and continue on toward PISA. You will probably want to stop in Pisa for a few pictures of the

Leaning Tower, but frankly Pisa is somewhat overrated. It is such a solid mass of tourists and souvenir shops during the summer season that you can hardly find a place to park before trying to squirm your way to the central piazza. Admittedly, the duomo, gleaming white with its companion leaning tower, is impressive, so if you have never seen it, do stop. But even more interesting and not nearly so "touristy" is the beautiful city of LUCCA located only a few kilometers to the north. This too is an ancient city, even more perfectly preserved than its neighbor, Pisa. An enormous wall surrounds the city, so wide that it even harbors pretty small parks and a road which runs along the top. A drive along the top of these ramparts is a wonderful way to get a bird's eye view of this extremely picturesque medieval town before you park your car and explore on foot.

Villa la Principessa
Lucca

As you are driving from Pisa to Lucca along the old road, there is a handsome villa just to your left, only about 4 kilometers before you arrive in Lucca. The VILLA LA PRINCIPESSA is a palace-style hotel set in a beautiful park with a pretty swimming pool (a welcome bonus after a long day of sightseeing). The inside of the villa could be considered somewhat flamboyantly decorated in terms of color schemes, but the setting is lovely and the building beautiful. The price tag is, however, a very expensive one, and if it does not suit your pocketbook, consider instead the BED & BREAKFAST OF TUSCANY in Montevettolini (page 176).

DESTINATION II   PORTOFINO

When you leave the Villa la Principessa, head back to the expressway and continue north.   What looks like a glacier shimmers white in the foothills of the Apuan Alps which rise to the right of the highway. This is not snow at all, but rather your introduction to the renowned white Italian marble. You might enjoy a detour to visit some of the marble mines. Exit the highway at CARRARA and take the winding drive up into the hills to the ancient village of COLONNATA - famous through the ages for its marvelous white marble. As you wander this tiny town you will be following the footsteps of the perfectionist, Michelangelo, who used to come to Carrara personally to choose huge blocks of marble from which to carve his masterpieces.

Leaving Carrara you will enjoy an adventure of an entirely different kind - exploring the five little isolated towns on the coast called CINQUE TERRE. This area is quickly becoming linked with civilization so do not tarry if you love the thrill of discovering old fishing villages still untouched by time.

To begin this portion of your journey take the small road from Carrara west returning to the main highway and continuing on to the port of LA SPEZIA, a large seaport and navy town.   From here you might want to take the short drive to the tip of the peninsula south of La Spezia to visit the old fishing village of PORTOVERERE which clings to the steep rocks rising from the sea. This was one of Lord Byron's haunts when he lived across the bay at San Terenzo. You will then need to return to La Spezia to continue your journey.

The Cinque Terre used to be five completely isolated fishing villages on a stretch of land between La Spezia to the south and Levanto to the north. First only a footpath connected these tiny villages, then a train was installed, and now real civilization is encroaching with a road under construction which will open them all to the world of tourism. Three of the towns are accessible now by road. From La Spezia you can travel to RIOMAGGIORE and then on to MANOROLA. From the northern approach of Levanto you can travel by road to the first town of MONTEROSSO. Still completely cut off from car traffic are the ancient fishing hamlets in between - VERNAZZA and CORNIGLIA. It is best to drive as far as possible from La Spezia stopping first at Riomaggiore and then on to Manorola. Upon arrival you can let your mood, the time, and the weather dictate your explorations. You can continue on by hiking the spectacular trails connecting the villages, by taking the small ferry between them, by using the train - or, best yet, by combining all these options. If you have time to see only one of the scenic towns, Vernazza, which clings perilously to a rocky promontory forming a tiny harbor, is perhaps the most scenic.

After Cinque Terre continue north along the coast. If you are in a hurry return to the freeway A 12. If time is not a problem, continue along the coast via the towns of SESTRI LEVANTE and CHIAVARI to SAN MARGHERITA. At San Margherita take the small road south for the short drive to the "picture book" village of PORTOFINO. This last section of the road, especially in summer, is jammed with traffic, but the plum at the end is worth the trials endured to reach it. Portofino is by no means undiscovered, but it is well-deserving of its accolades.

As you approach Portofino watch for the entrance sign for the HOTEL SPLENDIDO. There is a guard at the entrance and only those with reservations are allowed to follow the little road as it winds up the hill to the magnificent villa-style hotel. The Splendido is deluxe: a *super expensive* hotel whose prices include breakfast and dinner. But what a gorgeous setting. The hotel is perched in the hills above the town with splendid views of the sea and the harbor. A swimming pool and tennis courts nestle below the hotel and enchanting little paths thread their way through the gardens, offering strategically placed benches for quiet moments to savor the stunning view. It is an easy walk into Portofino if you can bear to leave this haven.

Hotel Splendido
Portofino

Portofino is considered an Italian national treasure and it truly *is* a jewel. Her tiny harbor is filled with gorgeous yachts, small ferries, and colorful fishing boats. In the center of town is a delightful small square. Enveloping the harbor are colorful tall and narrow fishermen's cottages painted in warm colors of sienna, ochre, and pink and all sporting green shutters. Bright flower boxes accent the windows and the laundry flaps gaily in the breeze. Vivid reflections of these quaint little houses shimmer in the emerald water. Beyond the town the heavily forested, beautiful green hills rise steeply to complete this idyllic scene.

NOTE: While staying in Portofino, if you appreciate gourmet dining, drive south to one of Italy's finest restaurants, the CA'PEO, located in Chiavari a Leivi. You must make prior reservations because Franco and his wife Melly only take guests who call ahead since the food is specially prepared depending upon how many will be dining: telephone (0185) 319090. The Ca'Peo, whose origins date back to a very old farmhouse, is located high in the hills overlooking the coast. Be forewarned, the meals *VERY* expensive, but the lodging rates are far more reasonable than at the Hotel Splendido, so if you enjoy fine food and wines and the price of dining is not a factor, you can visit Portofino instead of overnighting there and stay at the Ca'Peo which offers a limited number of suites. (See page 138.)

DESTINATION III   MILAN

DETOUR NOTE: For those of you travelling to the French Riviera, we wish you "adieu" in Portofino. From Portofino continue to follow the coastal highway west to Genoa along the Italian Riviera into the principality of Monaco and across the border to France.

For the rest of "our group", after leaving Portofino return to the main highway and continue west for about 29 kilometers to Genoa. Bypass Genoa and instead, as you circle the city, watch for the freeway A7 going north to Milan.

An interesting detour on the last leg of your journey is the PAVIA CARTHUSIAN MONASTERY (Certosa di Pavia). Probably the simplest way to find it would be to watch for the turnoff to Pavia (about 96 kilometers north of Genoa). At this point take the road east to Pavia and from there go north about 9 kilometers to the Carthusian Monastery. Lavishly built in the 15th Century, this splendid monastery is claimed by some to be one of the finest buildings in Italy. (Check carefully the days and hours open - it is usually closed on Mondays and for several hours midday.) The outside of the monastery is lavishly designed with colorful marble and intricate designs. Inside, the small cloisters are especially charming with 122 arches framed by beautiful terra cotta moldings. There is also a baroque fountain within, plus several small gardens. Next to the monastery you will find the former Palace of the Dukes of Milan which is now a museum.

After your tour of the monastery it is approximately 26 kilometers farther north to MILAN. Unfortunately, Milan does not offer a wealth of charming places to stay: most are modern, commercial hotels, seemingly way over-priced, with little old world ambiance. Our favorite, the Hotel et de Milan, is closed for renovations as this book goes to press, but will probably be open again in the fall of 1993. Until then, another well located place to stay is the Hotel Manzoni. From here, you can walk to the major sights and shopping - no need for taxis.

The outskirts of Milan are not much fun: frustrating traffic and not too pretty commercial buildings. But the heart of Milan has much to offer. If you enjoy shopping (and Milan has some of the finest in Italy), the splendid glass-domed shopping arcade, lined with beautiful boutiques and cozy cafes is outstanding. After a stroll through the arcade, you emerge into an imposing square dominated by the truly spectacular DUOMO, the third largest cathedral in the world. Not only is the size impressive, but this sensational cathedral has a multi-colored marble facade enhanced by over 100 slender spires piercing the sky. Also, a must to see is Milan's opera house. Every opera buff knows about LA SCALA. Even if you have not been an opera enthusiast in the past, if you are in Milan during the opera season (which usually runs from December to May) write ahead and try to get tickets - the theater is stunning and an experience not to be missed. When it is not opera season, there is usually some other performance or concert featured. If you haven't purchased seats in advance, you can try to buy them the day of the performance (the ticket office is located down a flight of stairs to the left of the opera house).

Rome to Milan via the Italian Riviera

Highlights of Southern Italy & Sicily

Rome

Anzio
Nettuno

Abbey of
Monte Cassino

Dubrovnik

Corfu &
Greece

Naples
Pompeii
RAVELLO
Salerno

Bari

Castellana Caves
ALBEROBELLO

Capri

Potenza

Matera

Taranto

Brindisi

Paestum

Sibari

TROPEA

Erice
Trapani
Marsala
Segesta
Selinunte
Agrigento

PALERMO
Cefalu
Enna
Piazza
Armerina

Messina
Villa San Giovanni
TAORMINA
Catania
Siracuse

◎ **OVERNIGHT STOPS**

Suggested Side Trips ━ ━ ━

77

Highlights of Southern Italy & Sicily

Having visited the famous trio of Rome, Florence, and Venice, most tourists think that they have "seen" Italy. If childhood geography lessons call forth such names as Pompeii, Herculaneum and Paestum, all too frequently the urge to visit these jewels of archaeological wonders is lost in the misconception that southern Italy is an uninteresting destination. What a waste. Southern Italy has fascinating ruins, gorgeous coastlines, beautiful medieval walled villages, lovely beaches, marvelous hilltowns, and some of the most unusual sights in Italy. Best yet, what fun to return home and casually mention to your dinner partner, who thinks he has been everywhere, that you think the Emerald Grotto on the Amalfi coast far exceeds the beauty of the Blue Grotto of Capri or that the Greek ruins at Paestum outshine many found in Greece or that you are still haunted by the mysterious town of Alberobello.

Therefore, for those of you who have already seen the fantastic highlights of northern Italy, we take pleasure in presenting to you the best of southern Italy. This itinerary makes a circle of southern Italy in order to suit the travel needs of a wide selection of tourists. Follow the entire route or select the portion best for you since this itinerary lends itself especially well for the traveller who wants to take only a segment. As an example, the journey from Rome to Brindisi is a popular one for the lucky tourist on his way to Greece. Or the west coast is a popular drive for the tourist who wants to visit Sicily and then return to Rome by air or ferry. And most popular of all is the segment from Rome to the Amalfi Drive. So, this itinerary allows you to custom tailor your journey and gives you many wonderful tips on what to see along the way.

ORIGINATING CITY   ROME

ROME is a most convenient starting point to begin a tour of southern Italy. Rome Airport is the destination of planes from all over the world and here passengers begin their "Roman holiday". In Rome you can immerse yourself in a wealth of history, art, architecture, museums, and monuments - and build a foundation for the sights which will be encountered on your journey southward.

Because there is such a wide selection of accommodations in Rome in various price categories and locations, it seems most practical for you to choose the hotel that best suits your personality and budget from the hotel description section in the back of this guide. You will find that Rome has many excellent hotels and, even though the city is large, most of the hotels are still within walking distance of both shopping and sightseeing highlights. Or, if you do not like to walk, ask the concierge at your desk to call you a taxi or direct you to the nearest subway station. (Rome's main subway line stretches across the city - conveniently connecting most of the places of interest for the tourist.)

When leaving the city by car, bear in mind that Rome always has a monumental traffic problem. Within the city look for strategically placed signs that indicate that there is a freeway ahead. It might be quite a distance, but be patient as these signs will lead you to the outskirts of Rome to the highway encircling the city. Follow the freeway around to the exit for the major expressway heading south, highway A2. When you reach this expressway continue south for approximately 128 kilometers to the exit for CASSINO. Actually you will be able to spot your destination from several miles away because the ABBEY OF MONTE CASSINO crowns the top of a large mountain to the left of the highway as you drive south. When you reach Cassino turn off the expressway and about midway through town the road that winds up the summit of the mountain to the Abbey of Monte Cassino is clearly marked. This abbey, founded by St Benedict in 529AD, is extremely interesting both religiously and historically. For war historians the abbey is very significant because this is where the Germans held out against the Allied forces for almost a year in World War II. When the mountain was finally conquered in May 1944 it opened the way for Allied forces to move into Rome. As you read your history books it seems strange that one fort could hold out for so long, but when you see the abbey you understand. It is an enormous building on the crest of a precipitous mountain. In the siege the abbey was almost destroyed but it has been rebuilt according to the original plans and is very impressive.

NOTE: For those of you who for sentimental or historical reasons are especially interested in World War II, there is another destination you might well want to visit in this day's journey. ANZIO is a town on the coast about 56 kilometers south of Rome and could easily be included as a stop before Cassino. It was at Anzio that the British and the Americans landed in January 1944. The emotional reminder of this terrible war is a few kilometers south at NETTUNO where 8,000 white crosses and stars of David range - row after row across the green lawn. There is a circular drive around the beautifully maintained, parklike grounds where you will also find a memorial chapel and small war museum. For those who lost family or friends during the invasion there is an office to the right as you drive in where you can find out exactly where your loved ones are buried.

From Cassino return to the expressway and continue south for about 59 kilometers until you see the sign for POMPEII. Unless you have absolutely NO interest in archaeology you must stop in Pompeii, the city of your childhood geography books, where time was frozen in the year 79 AD for the 25,000 people smothered by ashes from the eruption of Vesuvius. Some of the sites within Pompeii are still under repair from the destruction wrought by the mighty 1980 earthquake, but do not let this deter you. There is so much to see that you will never feel cheated by nature's mischief. (If you are a dedicated student of archaeology you must also visit the NATIONAL ARCHAEOLOGICAL MUSEUM in Naples where many of the artifacts from Pompeii are housed in a magnificent museum.)

Time slips eerily back 2,000 years as you wander the streets of Pompeii and visit the temples, lovely homes, wine shops, bakery, and public baths. There is probably no other place on earth where you can feel so strongly the pulse of ancient days. Many of the private homes have been reconstructed so you can marvel at the lovely inner courtyards, beautiful dining rooms in Pompeii-red with intricate paintings on the walls, fountains, servants' quarters, bath rooms, and gardens. At the entrance to Pompeii there are souvenir stands where you can purchase a guide book to the city, or, if you prefer, you can hire a private guide at the entrance. Pompeii is so fascinating that you might well want to come back to spend a complete day visiting the city and the nearby ruins of Herculaneum which are also very interesting.

Leaving Pompeii, head to the coast in the direction of Sorrento where the AMALFI DRIVE, one of the most beautiful stretches of coast in the world, begins. Be sure to time your journey when there is sufficient daylight because you will want to be sure to glimpse every magnificent vista as well as safely negotiate this extremely twisty and precipitous road.

There are many excellent choices for hotels along the Amalfi Drive. Concentrated in just a few kilometers are some of the most splendid hotels, both budget and luxury, in all of Italy. It is hard to recommend just one town along the way since each is unique. A favorite is the cliff-clinging village of RAVELLO, reached by a road which twists and winds its way up and up and up and then suddenly delivers you in a little village high in the clouds with absolutely dazzling views.

Hotel Palumbo
Ravello

In Ravello there are several wonderful inns - all of which can be heartily recommended, but none can surpass the delightful PALUMBO. You enter into a light and airy reception room brimming with flowers and sunlight. Tucked throughout the inn are cozy little nooks filled with antiques. The inside dining room is charming, but usually meals are taken outside to enjoy the surrounding scenery to the maximum: steep hills covered with vineyards flowing down to the rugged coast where brilliant blue water dances between the rocks. The garden terrace of the Palumbo is an oasis of beauty and quiet enhanced by spectacular views. On an upper level is a rooftop terrace where the sun and views are again offered for the lucky guest. The Palumbo is a real jewel.

Before leaving Ravello you will certainly want to visit some of the other small fishing villages which dot the coast, such as POSITANO and AMALFI. These towns during the season are bursting with tourists, but fun to see.

Also, if you have not been able to include an interlude on Capri during your Italian holiday it would be easy to arrange an excursion to this enchanted island from your location on the Amalfi coast. Steamers and hydrofoils depart regularly from Sorrento, Amalfi, and Positano. Ask at the tourist bureau or at your hotel for the schedule. (When the seas are rough it is more difficult to leave from Positano since there is no pier and it is necessary to take a small boat from the shore to the ferry.)

Also along the Amalfi coast is the EMERALD GROTTO, located between the towns of Amalfi and Positano. After parking, you buy a ticket and descend by elevator down the steep cliff to a small rocky terrace. Upon entering the water-filled cave, you will be rowed about the grotto in a small boat while your guide explains how the effect of shimmering green water is created by a secret tunnel allowing sunlight to filter from deep below the surface. The cave is filled with colorful stalactites and stalagmites which further enhance the mysterious mood. There is also a nativity scene below the water which magically appears and then drifts again from view.

DESTINATION II   ALBEROBELLO

When it is time to leave Ravello, there is an efficient expressway south to the "toe" of Italy. But for those who are en route to Brindisi or who have the luxury of time for another adventure, include a detour to the eastern coast, to the wondrous town of ALBEROBELLO.

Start early as there are several sightseeing stops recommended in route First of all, make the short side trip south to visit the spectacular ancient Greek city of PAESTUM. To reach Paestum take the Amalfi coastal road from Ravello to Salerno and then join the expressway for about 19 kilometers until the turnoff for Paestum which is located on a side road about a half-hour drive from the freeway. Magically, as soon as you go through the gates of the ancient city you enter a peaceful environment of a lovely country meadow whose grass is dotted with some of the world's best preserved Greek temples. As you walk the remains of the streets criss-crossing the city, your senses are thrilled by the sound of birds singing and the scent of roses. (Before leaving Paestum you might want to stop for a snack at the MARINI SEA GARDEN, a former villa set in a garden whose gates open onto the west side of the excavation).

When you rejoin the expressway, continue east for about 22 kilometers until the highway splits. At this point take the left branch heading east toward Potenza. About 112 kilometers beyond the branching of the highway, watch for the exit leading to the town of MATERA. Located about a half-hour drive north of the expressway, Matera is a strange, spooky, ghost town with a weird setting amongst ravines and deep gorges. The old town of Matera clings to the side of a hill crowned by a modern city. To visit the lower "lost city" whose crumbling buildings melt into the rocks is a fascinating experience.

From Matera continue on the road leading northeast to Alberobello. Here are some of the strangest structures in Italy - the TRULLI. These are circular stone buildings, usually built in small clusters, standing crisply white with conical slate roofs and whimsical twisted chimneys. Outside ladders frequently lead to upper stories. Often several of these houses are joined together to form a larger complex. The houses are intertwined with cobbled streets. What a strange and fascinating sight. These conical little houses form a jumble of a small village which looks as though it should be inhabited by elves instead of "real" people.

Trulli Houses

For a hotel choice, you should certainly choose the DEI TRULLI. This hotel is located on the outskirts of the trulli village and is made up of a cluster of ancient round houses. These conical dwellings have been made into guest cottages and are scattered around the large, park-like grounds, with pine tree lined paths leading between them. Each bungalow has a living room with fireplace, one or more bedrooms, a bathroom, and a small patio. One of the trulli houses has been transformed into the hotel dining room and another into the office. There is also a swimming pool and a tiny park with play equipment for children.

Hotel dei Trulli
Alberobello

The trulli houses are not confined to the town of Alberobello although this is where you will find them composing an entire village. In fact, the trulli houses you will see in the vicinity of Alberobello are sometimes more interesting than those in the town itself. As you drive along the small roads you will spot gorgeous villas cleverly converted from trulli houses that are now obviously the homes of wealthy Italians. Others are now farmhouses with goats munching their lunch in the front yard. Occasionally you will spot a charming old trulli home cozily nestled in the center of a vineyard. But most fun of all are the trulli homes of the free spirits. Their homes, instead of displaying the typical white exteriors, have been painted a brilliant yellow or pink or bright green with contrasting shutters.

As you are exploring the countryside around Alberobello you might want to take the short drive north to see the CASTELLANA CAVES where in a two-hour tour you will see many rooms of richly colored stalagmites and stalactites.

DESTINATION III　　　　　TROPEA

NOTE: Alberobello is about 72 kilometers from BRINDISI, the popular port from which to take the ferry to Corfu and on to Greece, and only about 56 kilometers from BARI which is the port to use for ferries to Dubrovnik. So, if your plans are to continue your travel adventures by boat, then Alberobello is most strategically positioned. In both Bari and Brindisi you can turn in your rental car if your holiday in Italy has ended.

However, for the rest of "our tour" the itinerary continues on to the exciting destination of Sicily. When you leave Alberobello take the road south to the coast. Stop to see the ancient port of TARANTO which is connected by a bridge to the modern city of Taranto. Even if you are not interested in ancient history you might enjoy seeing the Italian naval ships - giant grey monsters sitting in the protected harbor.

From Taranto continue along the arch of Italy's boot until you come to Sibari where there is a road leading east to join the main expressway. When you are again on the Highway A3 continue south for only a few kilometers until you come to the exit for the tiny spur which juts up from the toe of Italy's boot and continue along the coast toward the town of TROPEA, located near the point of the peninsula.

Baia Paraelios
Tropea - Parghelia

Just before Tropea, a sign on the right of the road points to the HOTEL BAIA PARAELIOS, a very special hotel which allows you to create the wonderful combination of a beach holiday with a sightseeing tour. The hotel is a cluster of cottages, cleverly spaced at various levels leading down to the beach. Each cottage has a sitting room and one or more bedrooms plus a private terrace. Although the hotel is not old, a definite "inn" feeling prevails. The small reception room at the crest of the slope has pretty prints on the wall, baskets of flowers, a few antiques, and the definite flavor of good taste. The cottages are quite appealing with tiled floors and earth tone colors. On a small terrace as you walk down to the beach is an inviting swimming pool. Other amenities include a beautiful creamy-white sand beach dotted with lounge chairs and a cheerful dining room with an outdoor terrace. Just a few kilometers beyond the hotel (which is officially located in the town of Parghelia) is Tropea, an ancient fishing village perched on the cliffs overhanging the brilliant blue sea.

Sicily

To Genoa
To Sardinia
To Tunis
To Naples
To Villa S. Giovanni
Messina
To Reggio
Erice
Trapani
Monreale
PALERMO
Ce Falu
Segesta
TAORMINA
To Tunis
Marsala
Castelvetrano
Enna
Selinunte
Catania
Piazza Armerina
Agrigento
Siracuse

Small roads
Expressways
Archaeological sites ▲

89

Sicily

You can end your holiday savoring the beauty of Italy's southern coast, enjoying the tranquil beauty of the deserted beaches and the inviting clear water. However, if you are still in the mood to travel, Sicily beckons, just a short drive and boat ride away. Sicily is a treasure of ancient monuments - a must for those who love archaeology. The continuation of this itinerary crosses the narrow channel leading from the tip of the toe over to the island of Sicily.

Upon leaving Baia Paraelios, return to the expressway and continue south the short distance to the tip of the toe and take the exit to Villa San Giovanni. The route to the ferry is clearly marked. The boat ferries leave at least twice an hour for MESSINA, Sicily. After buying your ticket, drive your car to the indicated lane and wait with all the trucks, campers and other cars for the signal to drive onto the boat. When on board you may leave your car and go upstairs to a lounge area where snacks can be purchased while traversing the short channel. In half an hour, the large ferry draws up to the pier in Messina and you drive off to experience some of the most beautifully preserved Greek ruins to be found anywhere in the world.

When the ferry arrives in MESSINA follow the freeway signs to TAORMINA, about a half-hour drive south. Once in town watch for signs to the SAN DOMENICO PALACE which commands a dramatic perch overlooking the sea. The San Domenico Palace is a museum-quality monastery which has been exquisitely converted into a deluxe hotel. Stunning antiques, appropriate to the period, are seen in every nook and corner. If you listen carefully, you can almost hear the soft chant of hooded monks quietly meditating as they walk through the arcaded courtyard. However, the superb amenities of today have been discreetly interspersed with the relics of the past and even a swimming pool now nestles in the garden.

San Domenico Palace
Taormina

The town of Taormina is enchanting, seemingly glued to the top of a small peninsula, it juts out to the sea and then drops steeply to the coast below. Quaint, colorful streets wind through the town where you can browse in the gift shops, visit small churches, enjoy a cappuccino at a little cafe, or simply enjoy the view.

DESTINATION V   PALERMO

From Taormina follow the freeway south toward CATANIA and PALERMO. Instead of going directly to Palermo you might want to take the approximately 128 kilometer round trip excursion south to SYRACUSE which is an ancient Greek city dating back to 700BC. The Greeks loved beauty and here overlooking a gorgeous blue bay they built their theaters, temples, and coliseums. Of special interest is an enormous theater over 400 feet across.

ENNA is about an hour's drive west from Catania. Should you want to include another short detour, about 32 kilometers south of Enna is the town of PIAZZA ARMERINA, about 6 kilometers southwest of which there are some excellent mosaics in the remains of an ancient Roman villa - the VILLA OF CASALE. Returning to Enna take the expressway north toward the coast and then head west to PALERMO.

Palermo is a large city with horrendous traffic and unsightly new construction. However, it makes a good base from which to explore some of the jewels of Sicily and luckily there is a splendid hotel here, the VILLA IGIEA GRAND HOTEL. Actually, the hotel is much more like a small castle than a villa and is an oasis in a bustling city. The hotel is located on the ocean right next to the harbor. The bedrooms are large and nicely furnished in a traditional motif and those in the rear have a lovely view over the back garden to the sea. There is a pool in the garden which even sports its own miniature Greek temple.

Villa Igiea Grand Hotel
Palermo

From Palermo there are many fascinating excursions. A circle trip from Palermo includes some of Sicily's finest archaeological sites. To begin your journey take the expressway west toward TRAPANI. About 8 kilometers after the highway splits you will see a sign for SEGESTA which is located only a few minutes from the expressway. Here in a remote mountain area stands a delightful Greek Doric temple - practically perfect in its preservation. In fact, many experts consider this to be one of the finest Greek Doric temples in the world today. But one of the most superb aspects of this temple is its location: there is nothing to jar the senses. Reached by a path leading up from the parking area, the temple is located on a small hill with great natural beauty all around. After visiting the temple return to the parking area and follow the signs up the hill for another treat - a small, but beautiful Greek theater. Again, the location is what makes this theater so special. What an eye the Greeks had for beauty. The stage is set in such a way that the spectators look out across the mountains to the sea.

Just north of Trapani is the ancient town of ERICE perched on rocks soaring over 2,000 feet in the clouds. This is a fascinating walled city filled with colorful medieval houses.

South of Trapani the road circles the island and passes through MARSALA which gives its name to the famous Marsala wine of the region.

The next destination is the great Greek ruins at SELINUNTE. As you near Castelvetrano watch for signs for the coastal archaeological site. Here by the ocean are the impressive remains of some of the most gigantic temples left by the Greeks. It is staggering to imagine how the Greeks, more than 2,500 years ago, could have pieced together the huge blocks of rock weighing over 100 tons each. From Selinunte the expressway heads directly north for your return to Palermo.

Another recommended side trip from Palermo is to visit the ancient fishing village of CEFALU built on a rocky peninsula about an hour's drive east from Palermo. Not only is this a very colorful fishing village complete with brightly hued boats and twisting narrow streets, but there is also a splendid Norman cathedral built by King Roger in the 12th Century in fulfillment of a promise to God for sparing his life during a storm at sea.

Two of Palermo's major sights are luckily only a few miles from the city. In MONREALE, about 8 kilometers south, is an awesome cathedral which is especially famous for its beautiful mosaic panels showing a strong Moorish influence. Reading from left to right these 130 pictures depict the complete cycle of both the Old and the New Testaments. The bronze doors of the cathedral are beautiful, designed by Bonanno Pisano, a famous 12th-century artist. The other sight close to Palermo is MONTE PELLEGRINO, just west of the city. Here is a cave which has been transformed into a chapel commemorating Santa Rosalia, a Duke's daughter who became a hermit - living and dying in this cave.

There is still another very important archaeological site on Sicily - the ruins of the VALLEY OF THE TEMPLES at ARRGRIGENTO. There is no doubt that this ancient Greek city, with the Temple of Juno, the Temple of Concord, the Temple of Hercules, the Temple of Jupiter and the Temple of the Dioscuri, is a marvelous example of the tremendous wealth, power and skills of the ancient Greeks. Because this excursion takes such a long drive of which only a short portion is freeway and because there is no excellent inn to recommend for the night, it seems that the wealth of temples that are more easily accessible will probably suffice for all but the most ardent ancient Greek enthusiast.

When it is time to leave Sicily, Palermo is a convenient gateway. From here you can fly to Rome and make a connection to your homeward flight or else you can take a ferry back to Naples, Genoa, Sardinia, or even Tunis.

Switzerland

Austria

4

2

Venice

3

● Milan

1

Yugoslavia

5

7

6 ● Genoa

France

● Florence

8

● Assisi

9

Corsica

10

● Rome

Sardinia

Naples ●

Bari ●

11

14

12

Key Map

Palermo ● Taormina ●

Sicily

97

13

BELLUNO

Vittorio

13   13

A27

A23   UDINE

56

San Floriano

YUGOSLAVIA

Asolo

47

248

Ponzano

348

53

Castel Franco

53

Cavasagra

TREVISO

13

A4

A4

A23

TRIESTE

Mogliano
Veneto

47

Torcello

PADUA

Dolo   Mira

Lido

VENICE

● Places to Stay
○ Orientation/
   Sightseeing

98

Map 1

AUSTRIA

AUSTRIA

49

49

Rasun

A22

MERANO

38

Lana

51

Sexton (Sesto)

38

BOLZANO (Bolzen)

Bressanone (Brixen)

Corvara

Vols (Fie)

48

CORTINA

42

42

Tiers (Tires)

48

51

Val d' Ega

48

Cavalese

51

A22

BELLUNO

● *Places to Stay*

○ *Orientation/ Sightseeing*

TRENTO

Pergine

47

50

Feltre

Map 2

Bolzano

A22

TRENTO

Pergine

47

45

RIVA

A22

45

Gargnano

Lake Garda

A22

Gardone

Desenzano

San Vigilio

BRESCIA

GARDA

A4

Milan

Sirmione

236

567

VERONA

A4

A4

Venice →

236

45

Cremona

- ● Places to Stay
- ○ Orientation/ Sightseeing

100

Map 3

SWITZERLAND

Valsoda -
San Mamete

LUGANO ○

Lake Como

VERBANIA
○

Lake Maggiore

STRESA ○

Isola dei
pescatori

Bellagio

●LECCO

Cernobbio

○ COMO

Erba
●

A9

○ *Bergamo*

Malpensa
Airport

A8

A4

A26

A4

MILAN ●

Linate
Airport

○ *NOVARA*

A7

A1

Maleo
●

● *Places to Stay*

○ *Orientation/*
Sightseeing

Cremona ○

PIACENZA ○

A21

Map 4

101

SWITZERLAND

● Champoluc

A4

FRANCE

Places to Stay ●
Orientation/ ○
Sightseeing

A26

A5

A4

Vercelli ○

A26

25

✈

Casale ○

590

457

TURIN
(Torino) ○

Moncalvo ○

● Sauze d'Oulx

A21

457

Cioccaro di
Penango ●

A21

Asti ○

○ ALESSANDRI

102

Map 5

590
Casale
Montcalvo
457
Cioccaro di
Penango
ASTI
A26
A21
ALESSANDRIA
A21
A21
A7

Maleo
A1
Cremona
PIACENZA
A1

A26
A7

● Places to Stay
○ Orientation/
   Sightseeing

A10
GENOA
A12
Camogli
PORTOFINO
Chiavari a Leivi
A12

Finale Ligure

Map 6

103

Places to Stay

Orientation/
Sightseeing

FERRARA

Moderna

CastelFranco

A1

A13

BOLOGNA

A14

A1

Forli

A12

67

Portico di
Romangna

Pieve di
Camaiore

Monsummano

A11

LUCCA

A11

FLORENCE

Montevettolini

Carmignano

PISA

2

A1

104

Map 7

FLORENCE

Empoli

67

Nord
Sud
San
Casciano

2

Bargino

Tavarnelle

Badia a
Passignano

San Donato

Greve

Panzano

2

222

Reggello

Incisa

Vággio

TUSCANY

Valdarno

408

A1

● Places to Stay
○ Orientation/
Sightseeing
◎ Exit from
Expressway

429

Poggibonsi

Radda

429

Gaiole

SAN GIMIGNANO

Castellina

Colle d' Val d'Elsa

Monteriggioni

San
Sano

222

408

Arezzo

68

San
Felice

Castelnuovo

Monte
San Savino

73

Pievescola

541

Pretale

SIENA

73

73

73

73

A1

Rosia

Map 8

TUSCANY

← *Florence*
A1

AREZZO

Monte
Savino

73

SIENA

326

A1

Val
d' Chiana
Bettolle

CORTONA

Polgeto

Umbertide

Sinalunga

15

Terontola

UMBRIA

Montefellonico

Lake
Trasimeno

15

PERUGIA

Pianello

San Gregorio

A1

Montepulciano

ASSISI

Chiusi
Chianciano

220

SPINA

Torgiano

A1

Mercatello

3

2

Fabro

Campello sul
Clintanno

Orvieto
exit

Todi

SPOLETTO

● *Places to Stay*

○ *Orientation/*
   Sightseeing

◎ *Exit from*
   Expressway

ORVIETO

Rome

A1

3

Lake
Bolsena

TERNI

106

Map 9

Map 10

Places to Stay

Orientation/
Sightseeing

A2

A30

A16

A16

A30

NAPLES

POMPEII

A3

SALERNO

Ischia

AMALFI *Ravello*

SORRENTO *Positano*

CAPRI

Map 11

Sicily

Map 12

Stromboli

Parghelia

TROPEA

Filicudi

Salina

Alicudi

Lipari

Vulcano

MESSINA

"Toe"
of Italy

MILAZZO

A20

REGGIO

TRAPANI

PALERMO

CEFALÙ

A19

113

A18

MARSALA

A29

Sicily

TAORMINA

A19

A19

189

640

ENNA

CATANIA

417

AGRIGENTO

114

SIRACUSE

115

115

● Places to S

○ Orientatio
Sightseein

Map 13

PORTO
CERVO

OLBIA

SASSARI

597

ALGHERO

131

131

NUORO

537

ORISTANO

SARDINIA

131

● Places to Stay

○ Orientation/
Sightseeing

CAGLIAR

CARBONIA

Map 14

There is a fascinating section in southeastern Italy with a collection of strange round white buildings with grey stone conical shaped roofs.   These ancient houses seem to be "left over" from some Moorish tribe which must have inhabited this part of Italy long ago.   These houses are called "trulli" and are usually seen in groups of two or three.   In the town of Alberobello there is actually a whole village of the conical little houses whose jumble of domed roofs, whitewashed walls, and crooked little chimneys creates a most unusual sight.   Fortunately there is a good hotel in the area that is located within walking distance of the trulli village.   Not only is its location excellent, but the hotel captures the mood of the area since it is constructed within some of the trulli houses. Small bungalows are scattered around a large park-like area connected by winding pathways under the pine trees. Each bungalow is actually a suite with a modern bathroom, a living room with fireplace, one or more bedrooms, and a private patio.   The suites are spacious but the decor quite simple.   The dining rooms and the reception area each occupy their own "trulli".   Within the grounds are a pool and children's play yard.   If you are on your way to Greece or Yugoslavia you will find the Hotel dei Trulli a convenient choice: very close to Brindisi and Bari, the two major ferry ports.

HOTEL DEI TRULLI
Manager: Luigi Farace
Via Cadore
70011 Alberobello, Italy
tel: (080) 9323555 fax: (080) 9323560
28 rooms: Lire 240,000
Open all year
Credit cards: AX VS
Swimming pool - small park
68 km NW of Brindisi, 55 km SW of Bari

The Villa Cipriani is just as I had envisioned in every dream of Italy: an old villa snuggled on a hill, her softly faded exterior emphasized by dark green shutters, masses of roses creeping over trellises, columns adorned with vines, lazy views over rolling green hills, faded ocher-colored walls half hidden by tall cypress trees dotting nearby hilltops, birds singing in the garden, the sentimental rhythmical peal of church bells, a pianist on the terrace playing old love songs, the fragrance of flowers drifting through the air like the finest perfume, a balmy night under the stars - perfection. My impression of a romantic paradise must not have been a unique experience for in the garden was a wedding party. A beautiful bride - a handsome groom; they had fallen in love at the Cipriani and had returned with family and friends from the United States for their marriage. The Villa Cipriani is located in Asolo, a charming, small, medieval, walled hill town less than two hours northwest of Venice. It has an atmosphere so delightful that Robert Browning chose it as a residence. And the home he chose? The Cipriani. Luckily, the home is now a hotel and you, too, can "live" in Asolo. Although the Villa Cipriani is a sophisticated, polished hotel, the warmth of reception is as gracious as in a small, family run inn: the manager, Giuseppe Kamenar, personally sees that all of his guests are properly pampered.

HOTEL VILLA CIPRIANI
Manager: Giuseppe Kamenar
Via Canova, 298
31011 Asolo, Italy
tel: (0423) 55444 fax: (0423) 52095
31 rooms: Lire 385,000
Open all year
Credit cards: all major
65 km NW of Venice, 14 km E of Bassano
U.S. Rep: CIGA, 800-221-2340

Asolo is a beautiful medieval town in the low lying hills northwest of Venice, dominated by castle ruins on the hillside above, and filled with charming streets, gothic arcades, and frescoed facades.   It is here in this magical town where one of our favorite hotels in Italy, the Villa Cipriani, is secreted in a garden just a short stroll from the center of the village.   But since the price tag at the Cipriani does not fit everyone's budget, it is wonderful to now be able to recommend an alternate choice, the Hotel Duse, which had been highly recommended to us by several readers.   We were eager to take a look and, when we did so, were pleasantly surprised: this little inn is indeed a "keeper".   The location is superb - right in the very center of town, surrounded by romantic little streets lined with elegant shops. The Hotel Duse's management is very personalized yet very professional - friendly, helpful, and eager to please in every way.   There is just a tiny reception lobby leading up to the guest rooms, which although not outstanding in their decor, are quite pleasant, each with a private bath, air conditioning, television, direct dial phone and mini bar.   All are adequately spacious and furnished exactly the same except for the color scheme - color coordinated fabrics with matching drapes, spreads and chairs, in reds, greens or blues.   The bathrooms are nicely equipped, modern and spotlessly clean.

HOTEL DUSE
Manager: Luigi Prudente
Via Browning, 190
31011 Asolo (TV), Italy
tel: (0423) 55241 fax: (0423) 950404
12 rooms: Lire 120,000
Open all year
Credit cards: all major
No restaurant in hotel, but many nearby
65 km NW of Venice, 14 km E of Bassano

One of the joys of researching a guidebook is to discover a "jewel" of an inn - it is rather like a treasure hunt.   Rarely though do we find an excellent hotel which we have not heard of previously.   However, the Country House, located on a small lane less than a kilometer from the lower gates into Assisi, is just such a find.   The inn is actually an ancient peasant's cottage which Silvana Ciammarvghi, the owner, has lovingly restored and transformed into a small pensione.   It is not surprising that the hotel is so loaded with charm, for Silvana loves antiques and has an eye for beautiful wooden chests, tables, chairs, mirrors and beds.   In fact, the first floor of this inn is an antique shop.   Most of the furniture in the house is for sale but, no problem: when a piece is sold, another takes its place from the shop downstairs. All of the rooms have style and taste.   When we first discovered the Antichita "Three Esse" Country House it had just opened, and each time we visit we find more improvements.   Rooms are now available in a new wing overlooking the terrace, but our preference is definitely for those in the original farmhouse which we think have more character and pretty views overlooking the countryside.   One asset never changes, the gracious owner, Silvana Ciammarvghi, who will be there to greet you.   She speaks excellent English and will be happy to welcome you to her "home" which is an ideal location for exploring Umbria.

ANTICHITA "THREE ESSE" COUNTRY HOUSE
Owner: Silvana Ciammarvghi
S. Pietro Campagna 178
06081 Assisi, Italy
tel: (075) 816363   fax: (075) 816363
12 rooms: Lire 95,000
Breakfast only served
Open all year
Credit cards: all major
177 km N of Rome, 26 km E of Perugia

The Hotel Subasio is located in Assisi with one wall forming part of the ancient square in front of the Basilica of St. Francis. In fact, the hotel is actually linked to the Basilica by an arched colonnade. The setting is marvelous, with the rear of the hotel facing the beautiful Umbrian countryside. On the lower level there are several delightful view terraces romantically shaded by vines. Many of the rooms also have splendid vistas over the Umbrian valley. Request one of the deluxe rooms with a balcony - these are delightful. The public rooms of the Subasio are pleasant, but rather stilted and formal. However, you will not be inside much anyway. The terraces are magic: to sit and watch the lovely fields mellow in the evening sun with that very special glow which is so characteristic of Umbria is certainly one of life's real pleasures. It is no wonder that many celebrities have chosen the Hotel Subasio for residence when visiting Assisi; such famous names as Charlie Chaplin and James Stewart grace the guestbook. Andrea Rossi personally oversees the management of the hotel and there is a friendliness in the air from the gentle maid who turns down your bed in the evening to the charming waiter who helps select your local wine with dinner.

HOTEL SUBASIO
Owner: Andrea E. Rossi
Via Frate Ella, 2
06081 Assisi, Italy
tel: (075) 812206   fax: (075) 816691
56 rooms: Lire 200,000
10 suites: Lire 300,000
Open all year
Credit cards: DC VS
177 km N of Rome, 26 km E of Perugia

For a moderately priced little inn just off the Piazza del Commune in the heart of Assisi, the Hotel Umbra is a wonderful choice.   If you are expecting a luxury hotel with fancy decor, this will not be the hotel for you: although the public rooms have accents of antiques and a cozy ambiance, they are "homey" rather than grand.   The bedrooms, although clean and fresh, are very basic in decor.   Nevertheless, because of the absolutely delightful small terrace at the entrance which is oozing with charm, the Umbra would have won our hearts, no matter what was within. You reach the Umbra by way of a narrow little alley leading off from the Piazza del Commune.   The entrance is through wrought iron gates which open to a tiny patio - a green oasis of peace and quiet where tables are set under a trellis covered with vines whose leaves provide shade and paint a lacy pattern of shadows.   From this intimate terrace there is a lovely view.   Some of the bedrooms, too, have a panoramic vista of the Umbrian hills and valley.   There is an attractive dining room and several small drawing rooms.   This small, family owned and managed hotel is a real asset to the wonderful medieval city of Assisi.

HOTEL UMBRA
Owner: Alberto Laudenzi Family
Via degli Archi 6-Piazza de Comune
06081 Assisi, Italy
tel: (075) 812240   fax: (075) 813653
26 rooms: Lire 122,000-170,000
Closed mid-January to mid-March
Credit cards: all major
Central location off main square
177 km N of Rome, 26 km E of Perugia

The Hotel Florence is a moderately priced hotel in the charming ancient port of Bellagio. The location is prime - right on the main square. Across the street by the lake is a little tea terrace where you can have a snack while watching the boat traffic. If you are lucky enough to snare a front room with a balcony, you can step out through your French doors and be treated to a splendid view of Lake Como. There is a small reception area and, down a few steps, an intimate lounge with a fireplace, beamed ceiling and chairs set around tiny tables. A staircase leads to a guest dining room with a fireplace and ladderback chairs and to the guest rooms. On our last visit we were pleased to find many of the guest rooms have been redone - many with antique furnishings. Ours was a very cheerful, bright corner room with French doors opening onto a terrace where lounge chairs were invitingly set for viewing the lake. Another new item: jazz music is played every Sunday in the newly redecorated bar. The hotel is owned by the Ketzlar family, who are real pros: the inn has been in their family for 150 years and is now managed by Mrs Freidl Ketzlar and her daughter, Roberta. They both speak excellent English and are extremely gracious. Bellagio is such an atmospheric little town that we are happy to be able to recommend a pleasant, well-run, moderately priced hotel.

HOTEL FLORENCE
Owner: Ketzlar Family
Piazza Mazzimi
22021 Bellagio (Lake Como), Italy
tel: (031) 950342 fax: (031) 951722
38 rooms: Lire 113,000-126,000
Open April 15 to October 15
Credit cards: MC VS
Village center, near ferry
Lakefront location
80 km N of Milan, 31 km NE of Como

The Grand Hotel Villa Serbelloni is certainly appropriately named.   It definitely is *GRAND*.   In fact, the public rooms are almost overwhelming, with intricately painted ceilings, gold mirrors, fancy columns, Oriental rugs, gilded chairs, heavy chandeliers, and a sweeping marble staircase.   The bedrooms are quite nice, although I did not think the decor outstanding.   However, the quality is superb: lovely percale sheets, soft down pillows, and large towels.   The service, too, is excellent.   Located in the gardens by the lake there is a large swimming pool.   If you prefer sightseeing or shopping to swimming, the colorful old port of Bellagio is just steps from the hotel.   If you tire of exploring the town of Bellagio, the ferry is only a few minutes away, or, if you want to be discreet, the concierge can arrange a special boat to pick you up at the private pier in front of the hotel.   Perhaps the original grandeur of the Grand Hotel Villa Serbelloni has faded a little, but if ornate elegance and the feeling of living in a masterpiece of a palace appeals to you, I think you will enjoy your stay here.   Pretend you are a guest at a weekend house party - given by royalty, of course.

GRAND HOTEL VILLA SERBELLONI
Owner: Rudy Bucher
Manager: Giuseppe Spinelli
22021 Bellagio, Italy
tel: (031) 950216 fax: (031) 951529
95 rooms: Lire 360,000 - 480,000
Open April 10 to October 20
Credit cards: All except AX
Sumptuous palace on Lake Como
Swimming pool
78 km N of Milan, 31 km NE of Como
U.S. Rep: Jacques de Larsay 800-366-1510

Although surrounded by a sprawling, uninteresting concrete metropolis, the center of Bologna shelters a fascinating maze of ancient twisting streets, arcaded passageways, marvelous shopping under porticoed walkways and some of the best food in Italy. There is not a large selection of hotels in the historical part of this expensive city, and after looking at what was available, we chose the one that best fits the criteria of this guide as the Corona d'Oro, a pleasant, well-managed small hotel in the heart of the medieval quarter. The inner courtyard dates from the 14th Century, and the rest of the building has grown in stages since then. Upon entering the lobby, a few steps beyond the reception desk the room opens out to an inner courtyard, now covered over with a skylight which rolls back to allow the room to return to its original open-air status on balmy days. An abundance of plants, soft cream-colored walls and a few nice paintings give a pleasant appeal. The guest rooms are individually decorated, mostly with modern furnishings, but with a touch of the traditional in the prints nicely displayed on the walls and the sedate colors chosen. A few of the guest rooms have small balconies or terraces for no extra cost, so it is a good idea to ask if one is available.

HOTEL CORONA D'ORO
Manager: Dr. Mauro Orsi
Via Oberdan, 12
40126 Bologna, Italy
tel: (051) 236456 fax: (051) 262679
35 rooms: Lire 330,000
Closed month of August
No restaurant in hotel, but many nearby
Credit cards: all major
Located in heart of Bologna

In 1550, King John of Portugal decided to give a little gift to the Emperor Ferdinand of Austria, so he purchased an elephant in India, shipped it to Genoa, then planned to "walk" it to Austria.   This giant beast grew weary about the time it reached Bressanone and was stabled for two weeks at the Am Hohen Feld Inn. Young and old came from miles around to see this impromptu "circus".   The proprietor of the Am Hohen Feld was obviously a master at marketing: to maintain the fame of his establishment, he promptly renamed his hotel - you guessed it - the "Elefant".   A picture of our friend the elephant was painted on the front of the building commemorating the sensational event.   But even without an elephant story this hotel is a winner.   Although the bedrooms themselves are a little drab, they are immaculately clean and comfortable.   In contrast to the simplicity of the bedrooms, the reception areas and dining rooms are fantastic, incorporating beautiful antiques, museum quality paintings and magnificent paneling.   But, even if there were no elephant story nor an antique ambiance to the hotel, the Elefant would have another tremendous attribute: the food is fantastic.   Most of the eggs, butter, milk, fruit, and vegetables, and even the wine, come from the hotel's own farms.   Note: Bressanone is called Brixen on some maps.

HOTEL ELEFANT
Owner: Hotel Elefant, Inc
Manager: K.H. Falk
Via Rio Bianco, 4
39042 Bressanone (Brixen), Italy
tel: (0472) 32750 fax: (0472) 36579
43 rooms: Lire 200,000
Open March to November & Christmas
Credit cards: VS
Swimming pool
40 km NE of Bolzano, near Brenner pass

The Peralta is special - very special - not really a hotel at all, but rather a miniature medieval village tucked high in the coastal hills northeast of Pisa.   This cluster of buildings had fallen into ruin when the famous Italian sculptress, Fiore de Henriquez, discovered the village, fell in love, and decided to bring the hamlet back to life.   Fifteen years of reconstruction has resulted in a dream of a retreat.   Fiore de Henriquez has her home and studio in one of the buildings - the others now house the few lucky guests who find their way to this secluded paradise.   This hotel is definitely not for everyone.   Those who like a slick hotel with the assurance that everything will always work perfectly had best find other accommodation.   There are no promises here that there will never be a shortage of water or problems with the electrical power.   But this is a small price to pay for those of you who love to walk through groves of chestnut trees, pick wild flowers along secluded paths, read a favorite book while soaking in the sunshine or, best yet, do absolutely nothing at all except enjoy the breathtaking view out over the valley to the sea.   There is no planned activity at the hotel except for the camaraderie of fellow guests. However, if you want to do a little sightseeing, the Peralta is well located. Florence is only about 90 minutes away, Lucca (one of our favorite of Italy's walled cities) is about a half an hour's drive, Carrara (where Michelangelo came to hand-pick marble for his masterpieces) just a short excursion to the north and the seaside town of Viareggio close by.   Although the concept of the Peralta is rustic, it far surpassed what I had expected.   Although the rooms are simple, there is an elegance to their simplicity.   Obviously the talents of Fiore de Henriquez were called upon in the design and decor - each room abounds with rustic charm, with extensive use of handmade tiles, what appear to be hand-loomed fabrics and attractive wooden beds and chests.   Especially appealing is the tiny lounge where comfy sofas are grouped around a cozy fireplace.   You will also be delighted to discover, tucked high on a tiny plateau above the hotel, a swimming pool with a terrace where guests can enjoy a splendid view to the sea.

Many of the guests are British - probably because all the space at the hotel is controlled by a travel agency in London. Most of the staff are also from Britain, and those I met were exceptionally friendly and fun. Since it is the staff's day off on Thursday, there are no arrivals scheduled for that day. Whatever day you do arrive, be sure you have a reservation. The hotel is really secluded and you will certainly not want to take a long drive only to discover the hotel is full - which it usually is. When you make your reservation, you will receive a map with directions on how to get to the Peralta. However, should you be arriving prior to receiving a map, this will help: drive to Camaiore (just north of Lucca) then watch for a sign to Pieve di Camaiore. You will wind up in the trees where occasionally you will spot, if you look carefully, a few handwritten signs to the Peralta, giving encouragement that you are not lost. Don't give up. Just keep driving as the road twists and becomes narrow and steep and then ends ... at which point you park your car and continue on foot for the last quarter mile. (Leave your luggage in the car and someone will retrieve it for you later.) I assure you the journey is worthwhile.

PERALTA
Manager: Philip Harrison Stanton
Pieve di Camaiore, Lucca, Italy
tel: (0584) 951230
14 rooms: 81 English pounds
Rates include breakfast & dinner
Open Easter to October
No arrivals on Thursdays
Credit cards: none accepted
Res: Harrison Stanton & Haslam Ltd
25 Studdridge St, London SW6 3SL
tel: London (01) 7365094 fax: (01) 3842327
No children under 16
Swimming pool
35 km NE of Pisa, 18 km NW of Lucca

The Cenobio dei Dogi was formerly the summer home of the Genoese Doges, so it is no wonder that it has such an idyllic location nestled on a small hill which forms one end of Camogli's miniature half-moon bay. From the hotel terrace there is an enchanting view of the tiny cove lined with marvelous narrow old fishermen's cottages painted in all shades of ochers and siennas. The hotel has a very nice swimming pool, plus a private (though pebbly) beach. Many of the bedrooms have balconies which boast romantic views of this storybook scene. For tennis buffs, there is a tennis court, although I cannot imagine anyone wanting to play tennis with all the beautiful walking trails which make enticing spider web designs on the peninsula. Although the Cenobio dei Dogi is larger than most hotels which appear in this guide and its decor does not radiate antique ambiance, it possesses a solid, comfortable, no-nonsense kind of charm. It is not chic in the "jet set" style of hotels frequently found on the Riviera, but if you relate to gorgeous flower gardens, exceptional views, and slightly faded, "old world" comfort in one of the most picturesque villages in Italy, then I think you will love this hotel.

HOTEL CENOBIO DEI DOGI
Manager: Franco Orio
Via Nicolo Cuneo, 34
16032 Camogli, Italy
tel: (0185) 770041 fax: (0185) 772796
89 rooms: Lire 296,000-390,000
Closed January and February
Credit cards: all major
Former Doges' summer palace
Pool, private beach, tennis
Near Portofino - Italian Riviera
20 km SE of Genoa, 14 km NW of Portofino

The Albergo Vecchio Molino is a 15th-century mill which has been cleverly converted into an inn. Although it is very close to the busy highway that runs between Assisi and Spoleto, once you wind off the road and down the lane to this small inn, you drop out of the modern-day world and slip back into the tranquility of days long past. The mill has been meticulously renovated with taste and style, retaining its original massive stone walls, heavy wooden beams, vaulted ceilings and even the old wooden gears and giant grindstone. Best of all, the river still wraps itself around the mill, a constant reminder of the building's origins. Perched on the hillside above the inn, a 14th-century stone church with handsome columns gives the impression of a Greek temple just a short walk away. Inside, the inn is nicely furnished using many antiques whose dark wood handsomely sets off stark white walls. The bedrooms we saw were not large, but appealingly furnished using antique beds and chests. The decor throughout the inn lends an air of uncluttered sophistication. On the day we arrived, we had the impression that not many Americans stay at the inn and that perhaps there might not be an especially warm welcome to English speaking visitors. But we always have a soft spot for old mills and could not bear to leave this one out ... please give us some feedback.

ALBERGO VECCHIO MOLINO
Owner: Anna Maria Flagiello
Manager: Clememtimi Massimo
Via del Tempio
06042 Campello sul Clintunno (Spoleto), Italy
tel: (0743) 521122
17 rooms: Lire 175,000
Open April 1 to November 1
Credit cards: all major
141 km N of Rome, 11 km N of Spoleto

The newly-renovated Hotel Flora in the center of Capri is truly a delight. Just beyond the landmark Quisisana Hotel is the stark white building reflecting the sun's rays and trimmed with lush deep purple bougainvillea vines. Signora Vuotto runs her hotel with great care and attention - striving to make her guests feel the Hotel Flora is their "home away from home". She has succeeded. The small 24-room hotel has become known above all for its impeccable yet friendly service. The prim dining room with its smart striped yellow and green armchairs and colorful ceramic plates lining the walls, opens out to a large terrace overflowing with potted Mediterranean flowers and miniature palms. Guests linger over their morning cappucino to take in the view over the San Giacomo ancient monastery to the sea from cushioned wicker chairs. Chef Antonello practices his culinary expertise for dinner guests. There is a fresh, perfumed air about this elegant jewel of a hotel which is carried out through the luminous bedrooms and suites finely decorated with antiques, and colorful Pierre Deux fabrics. Each of the bedrooms has television, a small refrigerator and, best of all, a terrace with a view of the famous "Faraglioni" rocks. Spotless bathrooms are tiled in typical Caprese style. A swimming pool, soon to be completed, will be a welcome addition.

HOTEL FLORA
Owner: Virginia Vuotto
Via Federico Serena, 26
80073 Capri (NA), Italy
tel: (081) 8370211   fax: (081) 8378949
24 rooms: Lire 230,000 - 350,000
7 suites: Lire 400,000-500,000
Restaurant: Breakfast and dinner served
Open Easter - October
Credit cards: all major
Island of Capri, ferry from Sorrento or Naples

The Grand Hotel Quisisana conjures up the image of a Hollywood setting where the jet-set gather. The women, adorned in jewels and the latest swimming ensembles, sit in the sun and gossip about the latest scandal while their husbands (or boyfriends?) sit pool-side drinking Scotch and playing the game of grown boys - discussing their latest business ventures. But it is all great fun and quite in the mood of Capri which has been a playground for the wealthy since the time of the early Romans. The Grand Hotel Quisisana is a deluxe hotel with a gorgeous oval pool overlooking the blue Mediterranean. The air of formal elegance appears as soon as you enter the lobby decorated with marble floors, soft green velvet chairs, Oriental carpets, ornate statues, crystal chandeliers and beautiful paintings. All the bedrooms are well appointed and the deluxe rooms even have separate "his" and "hers" half-baths. Room rates include breakfast and lunch or dinner and you can choose from almost anything on the menu. The Grand Hotel Quisisana most definitely provides a setting and atmosphere to reflect the image of, and cater to, their jet-set clientele.

GRAND HOTEL QUISISANA
Manager: Gianni Chervatin
Via Camerelle, 2
80073 Capri, Italy
tel: (081) 8370788 fax: (081) 8376080
150 rooms: Lire 500,000
Open April through October
Credit cards: all major
Indoor & outdoor pools, sauna, tennis
Island of Capri, ferry from Sorrento or Naples
U.S. Rep: LHW
Rep tel: 800-223-6800

The Hotel Luna savors one of the most beautiful locations on the Island of Capri. It is just a short walk from the main town yet, in atmosphere, it seems miles away from the bustle and noise. The hotel is perched on the cliffs overlooking the spectacular coastline of green hills that drop straight into the sea and from which emerge giant rock formations. There is an outside terrace for dining which captures this view, and the premium rooms have balconies overlooking the sea. Just a short stroll from the hotel there is a very large pool surrounded by flowers which also has a splendid view. The decor of the hotel seems to be in need of refreshing. The overstuffed chairs and velvets and heavy furniture seem to conflict with the natural splendor of the landscape. However, the cliff-top setting is so lovely that we think the hotel is one of the best on Capri. The overall mood at the hotel is set by its delightful approach, a covered trellis pathway which, in summer, is completely shaded by brilliant bougainvillea and grape vines and bordered by flowers: a wonderful introduction to the Hotel Luna and to a restful interlude by the sea.

HOTEL LUNA
Managers: Mr/Mrs Strina & Mrs Vuotto
Via Matteotti, 3
80073 Capri, Italy
tel: (081) 8370433　fax: (081) 8377459
48 rooms: Lire 360,000
Open April to October
Credit cards: all major
On cliff above the sea
Pretty views & lovely pool
Island of Capri, ferry from Sorrento or Naples

The Villa Brunella is a small jewel located on the most picturesque and peaceful street of Capri, the Tragara, only a 10-minute walk to the center of town. The modern hotel, overlooking the Marina Piccola, squeezes the greatest advantage from its narrow, very deep lot. The hotel is built on levels starting at the street level with the terrace restaurant and "stepping down" the steep hillside to the blue swimming pool - at this point, only halfway down to the sea level (the beach is only about a 5-minute walk down the hill). The hotel is run more like a private home than a commercial hotel. The ever-gracious Vencenzo and his wife Brunella take great pleasure in entertaining guests and making them feel welcome. The 20 bedrooms, each with private bath, telephone, frigo-bar and air conditioning, are tastefully put together with pretty pink or powder blue floral bedspreads and matching curtains. The cool ceramic tiled floors, creamy white walls and potted plants add to the charm. Decoration in the rooms is really superfluous as the eye can hardly be torn away from the spectacularly dramatic views of the sea and island from one's own terrace. Simply heavenly.

VILLA BRUNELLA
Hosts: Vincenzo and Brunella Ruggiero
Via Tragara 24
80073 Capri (NA), Italy
tel: (081) 8370122 fax: (081) 8370430
20 rooms: 220,000-260,000
  Suites Lire 280,000-330,000
Restaurant: All meals served
Open: Easter - October
Credit cards: all major
Swimming pool, gardens, superb views
Island of Capri, ferry from Sorrento or Naples

If you are approaching Florence from the west, perhaps on your way from Milan to Florence, we highly recommend stopping en route, just before you reach Florence, at the Paggeria Medicea.   The hotel's address is Artimino, but the town is so small that I doubt you will find it on any map, so mark Carmignano instead on your map and when you arrive there you will find signs to Artimino, only a few minutes' drive farther on.   The hotel is cleverly incorporated into what were once the pages' quarters for the adjoining 16th-century Medicea villa "La Ferdinanda".   The long, narrow structure has been cleverly restored, preserving the many original chimneys which adorn the heavy, red-tiled roof.   An open corridor whose heavily beamed ceiling is supported by a stately row of columns forms a walkway in front of the rooms.   All of the guest rooms are simple, but very inviting, with tiled floors, pretty prints on the white walls, hand-loomed-looking white drapes hanging from wooden rods above the windows, and attractive antiques or copies of antiques as accents in each room.   There is a snack bar in the same wing as the hotel, but the main restaurant, Biagio Pignatta (which serves simple but delicious Italian cooking), is located in a nearby building which at one time housed the butler for the villa.   If you are a guest at the hotel, you have access to a delightful small Etruscan museum situated in the vaults of the adjoining Medicea villa "La Ferdinanda".

PAGGERIA MEDICEA
Manager: Alessandro Gualtieri
Viale Papa Giovanni XXIII
50040 Artimino, Italy
tel: (055) 8718081 fax: (055) 8718080
37 rooms: Lire 230,000
Open all year
Credit cards: all major
Swimming pool, tennis courts
20 km SW of Florence, 15 km S of Prato

The Villa Gaidello Club is located in the Emilia-Romagna, a region renowned for its cuisine - considered by many to be the finest food in Italy. Whether this is true or not, I do not know, but without a doubt the delicious pasta prepared by Paola Giovanna Bini (the owner) of the Villa Gaidello Club was the best I have *EVER* tasted. Paola Giovanna Bini, who inherited the farm from her grandmother, assumed the awesome task of reconstructing the 250-year-old farm house and adding three apartments (suites) which have been restored and decorated with care, keeping in mind the original character of the country home. These suites vary in size, accommodating from two to five persons. There are three suites in all: one accommodates 2-3 persons, one accommodates 3-4 persons, and one accommodates 4-5 persons. Although the rooms are pleasant, it is the food which makes this inn so very special: only the freshest vegetables and fruits are served; all the pasta is prepared the same day; the wines come from the farm's own vineyard; even the liqueur served after the meal is made from walnuts picked from the orchard. However, Paola Bini wants me to stress that it is *ABSOLUTELY NECESSARY* to make reservations for the restaurant: time is needed to prepare the food - all of which is strictly prepared the same day by hand.

VILLA GAIDELLO CLUB
Owner: Paola Giovanna Bini
Via Gaidello, 18
41013 Castelfranco Emilia, Italy
tel: (059) 926806 fax: (059) 926620
3 apartments: Lire 138,000 for 2 persons
Credit cards: none accepted
26 km W of Bologna, 13 km E of Modena

We happened upon this newly opened inn during our latest exploration of Italy's glorious Tuscany region, well known for its rolling, vineyard covered hills.   Just as the road curved into the small town of Castellina in Chianti, we noticed an inn we had never seen before and stopped for an inspection at the Albergo il Colombaio. The building is very old - probably at one time a farmer's home with its typical heavy tiled roof, thick walls and courtyard.   This comfortable inn is owned by the Baldini family and Roberta Baldini, the gracious daughter, is the manager.   She speaks very good English and gave us a complete tour of the small hotel.   The guest rooms are quite inviting, many with wrought iron beds and antique accents giving an appealing country flavor.   The 15 guest rooms and one suite all have private bathrooms and are fresh and pretty.   The dining room is especially cozy, again decorated with a rustic motif in keeping with the Tuscany countryside.   A continental breakfast is the only meal served here, but Roberta is happy to recommend a good local *ristorante* for dining.   On hot summer days, a great bonus is the swimming pool located on a terrace behind the inn.   For a reasonably priced place to stay, fresh and new, yet with an old-world ambiance, the Albergo il Colombaio is a welcome addition to the Tuscany region.

ALBERGO IL COLOMBAIO
Owner: Baldini Family
Via Chiantigiana, 29
53011 Castellina in Chianti, Italy
tel: (0577) 740444
15 rooms: Lire 110,000
Closed month of November
Credit cards: MC VS
Swimming pool
21 km N of Siena on road #222
50 km S of Florence

I visited the Pensione Salivolpi with the idea of including it only in our guide featuring inexpensive places to stay. However, the hotel is so very pleasant, that for those of you looking for a "budget" hotel while roaming the Tuscany hills, we have included this small, attractive pensione. Although the address is Castellina in Chianti (in the heart of the famous Chianti wine region), you will actually find the hotel on the outskirts of town, on the left-hand side of the road leading from Castellina to the small town of Sant Donato. The old, weathered stone farmhouse sits almost on the road. It is only when you pull into the parking area that the lovely position of the inn is revealed - behind the main building there is a beautiful view terrace featuring a lovely large swimming pool. The bedrooms are pleasant, reflecting the nice taste of the Salivolpi family. Previously when I dropped by to visit the Pensione Salivolpi, I could not find anyone who spoke English, however, I now understand that all the secretaries do speak English. With Florence only 40 minutes north and Siena 30 minutes to the south, the Pensione Salivolpi provides a simple, but very pleasant, base of operation.

PENSIONE SALIVOLPI
Owner: L. Salivolpi
Via Fiorentina - Loc. Salivolpi
53011 Castellina in Chianti, Italy
tel: (0577) 740484 fax: (0577) 741034
19 rooms: Lire 93,500
Open all year
Credit cards: MC VS
No restaurant
Swimming pool
21 km N of Siena on road #222
50 km S of Florence

The Tenuta di Ricavo is unique.   It is not a "hotel" at all in the usual connotation, but rather a tiny village with peasants' cottages which have been transformed into delightful guest rooms.   The stables are now the dining room and the barn is now the office.   You enter the park like setting through a huge pine forest where small cottages are nestled in amongst the trees.   Gardens are everywhere and roses embellish the weathered stone cottages giving them a fairy-tale appearance.   The total effect is absolutely enchanting.   Originally the village was the summer residence of a Swiss family who used it for holidays and later transformed it into an exquisite resort.   The family seeks no publicity.   They do not need it: the hotel is always filled with fortunate guests who have discovered this paradise.   However, the Tenuta di Ricavo is not for everyone. It is quiet. It is remote. It is unstructured.   But it is a haven for the traveller for whom a good book, a walk through the forest, a swim in the pool, a drink at sunset with fellow guests, and a delicious dinner are fulfillment.

TENUTA DI RICAVO
Owner: Lobrano-Scotoni Family
53011 Castellina in Chianti, Italy
tel: (0577) 740221 fax: (0577) 741014
25 rooms: Lire 220,000-340,000
Open April to mid-October
Credit cards: none accepted
Unique village hotel - 3 day minimum
Pool and 300-acre park
In the Tuscany Hills
21 km N of Siena on road 222
50 km S of Florence

Of the many magnificent old villas dotting the countryside near Venice, some have fallen into disrepair, some are still maintained as private residences, and a few have been converted into hotels. We looked at many of these fascinating villa-hotels but because of the expense of maintaining them, many are just too shabby to include. One however, the Villa Corner della Regina, still has an elegant, though slighted faded, appeal. Once home to Caterina, Queen of Cyprus, the villa dates from the beginning of the 16th Century and was later reconstructed around 1700 in the well-known Palladian style. It is set in extensive manicured formal gardens and surrounded by vineyards. A pool is located to the left of the main building while the wing to the right, which originally housed the stables, has been converted to guest rooms and also some time-share condominiums. The decor in the side stable annex is nothing special, just standard hotel-like furnishings, but the suites in the villa abound with antiques - very grand and ornate, even somewhat overly fussy for my taste. There are several dining rooms in the villa: my favorite is a charming room with salmon-colored marble walls enhanced by color-coordinated tablecloths and draperies - formal yet cozy and not the least bit intimidating. The food served at the villa is excellent and the wines are produced on the estate. Note: Cavasagra is located between the towns of Ospedaletto and Albaredo on the Hallwag map.

VILLA CORNER DELLA REGINA
Owner: Count Dona delle Rose
Via Corriva, 10
Near Ospedaletto
31050 Cavasagra, Treviso, Italy
tel: (0423) 481481 fax: (0423) 451100
23 rooms, 7 suites: Lire 150,000-400,000
Credit cards: all major
16th-century villa, swimming pool, large garden
45 km NW of Venice, 3 km W of Ospedaletto

A book on the most charming hotels in Italy could not be complete without including one of the queens of the world, the Villa d'Este. Originally the hotel was a private villa built in 1568 by the Cardinal Tolomeo Gallio. He obviously had elegant (and expensive) taste, for the Villa d'Este is truly a fantasy come true. From the moment you enter the enormous lobby with the sweeping staircase, marble, crystal, soaring ceilings, statues, and columns surround you. Everything is elaborate and ornate. The bedrooms are all elegantly furnished - no two are alike, but all are beautiful with color-coordinated carpets, wall-coverings and bedspreads. Some of the bedrooms have prime locations overlooking the lake. Although the interior is lovely, it is the outside where the fun really begins. The hotel opens onto a large terrace where guests relax with refreshing drinks. Just a short distance beyond the terrace is the lake where there is a dock for boats and a very large swimming pool which extends out over the water. Across the road from the hotel there are eight beautiful tennis courts and within the nearby area are seven golf courses. However, the most stunning feature of the Villa d'Este is its prime lakeside location and its park with lovely pathways winding between trees, a jogging course, glorious flowers, statues, and formal gardens.

VILLA D'ESTE
Manager: Mario Arrigo
22010 Cernobbio, Italy
tel: (031) 511471   fax: (031) 512027
158 rooms: Lire 600,000-696,000
Open April to November
Credit cards: all major
Pool, tennis, squash and gym
Swimming, windsurfing, waterskiing
53 km N of Milan, 5 km N of Como
U.S. Rep: LHW, 800-223-6800

The Anna Maria is located in Champoluc which is a small town at the end of the beautiful Ayas Valley which stretches north into the Alps almost to the Swiss border in northwest Italy. As you drive through the town of Champoluc you will see a small sign for the Anna Maria on the right side of the road just before you leave town. Turn right on this little lane which winds up the hill and look for the Anna Maria on your right, set in a serene pine grove. The Anna Maria is not a luxury hotel, but rather an old mountain chalet which is now a simple, but very charming, inn. A large deck for sunning stretches across the entrance. Inside there is a lovely dining room - my favorite room - which exudes warmth and coziness with its wooden Alpine-style country chairs, wooden tables, and gay red checked curtains at the windows. Upstairs the bedrooms are not luxurious but most inviting, with wooden paneling on the walls and a rustic ambiance, and each one with a private bathroom. Perhaps the most winning feature is Anna Maria, the owner, who is your hostess and oversees her little inn with a gracious charm. The atmosphere is "homey" - not for the fussy but wonderful for those who love the friendliness of a country inn in a mountain village.

ANNA MARIA
Owner: Anna Maria
Via Croues, 5
11020 Champoluc, Italy
tel: (0125) 307128
20 rooms: Lire 120,000
Open Jun 20-Sep 15; Dec 10-Apr 15
Credit cards: VS
Mountain location - NW Italy
175 km NW of Milan, 100 km N of Turin

The Ca'Peo, a well known restaurant serving some of the finest food in Italy, is located high in the coastal hills south of Genoa. You might think you will never arrive as the road winds ever upward through groves of olive and chestnut trees. But the way is well signposted, and just about the time you might be ready to despair, you will find a wonderful old farmhouse, owned by Franco Solari, who is host and in charge of the wines, and his wife, Melly, who is the chef. As we checked in, the entire family was in the kitchen busily chopping vegetables, rolling out pastry and preparing the fish for the evening meal. The dining room, enclosed on three sides by large arched windows, takes advantage of a sweeping view to the sea. Be aware that the meals are *VERY* expensive, but if you appreciate fine food and wines, superb. Dining is definitely the main feature; however, in a modern annex there are five suites available for guests who want to spend the night. The decor here is not antique, but each of the large suites is pleasant, and after lingering over a wonderful meal accompanied by delicious wines, how nice to walk just a few steps to your bed. A final note: the Ca'Peo is only about half an hour's drive from the popular resort of Portofino, so you might want to stay here instead or at least treat yourself to a memorable meal - but call ahead as reservations are necessary.

CA'PEO
Owners: Franco & Melly Solari
Via dei Caduti, 80
16040 Chiavari a Leivi, Genoa, Italy
tel: (0185) 319696 fax: (0185) 319671
5 suites: Lire 160,000
Closed November
Credit cards: VS
Gourmet restaurant (closed Mondays)
6 km N of Chiavari toward Leivi
44 km SE of Genoa, 22 km NE of Portofino

I was puzzled to receive a hotel questionnaire response postmarked St Simon's Island, Georgia. But quickly all was explained. It was from James Adams who had been living in Europe, perfecting his Italian cooking skills at one of the finest restaurant-hotels in Italy, the Locanda del Sant'Uffizio - Ristorante da Beppe. The owner, Giuseppe Firato ("Beppe"), speaks no English so when our request for information arrived, he asked his American protégé to respond. After visiting the hotel, I can only say that it was more perfect than anticipated. Below is James' wonderful letter describing so superbly his "home away from home".

"Originally in the 1500s the Locanda del Sant'Uffizio was a Benedictine monastery and served as such up until the mid 1800s after which time it passed into private hands serving as a farm. In 1972, Signore Giuseppe Firato (Beppe), a man from the village, bought the farm and slowly began converting it into its present form. Naturally at first there were only several rooms while the rest of the buildings were used for farming and wine growing. Through the years rooms have been added very carefully, with great respect for the traditional aesthetics, and now there are 35 guest rooms. All furnishings are antique and every detail of the decor has been rigorously overseen personally by Signore Beppe and his wife, Carla, with the result being a very tasteful, elegant, yet relaxed hotel cozily nestled amongst the vineyards in the hills of Monferrato. Other features include a tennis court, a swimming pool (in front of which one can have breakfast and lunch in the warm months) and, last but not least, there is the Ristorante da Beppe, an exquisite restaurant serving the finest of Piemontese cuisine. It is of course owned and operated by the Firato family, and, in fact, the restaurant preceded the hotel. It has earned one Michelin star and has been rated highly in notable Italian guides such as Espresso and Veronelli. When one combines the charm and relaxation of this elegant hotel with the pleasures of such a refined table, one is left with a very memorable experience."

There are many features that make the Locanda del Sant'Uffizio very special, but, without a doubt, the Firato family is responsible for the ambiance of warmth and hospitality which radiates throughout the hotel. Signore Beppe was born in the tiny village (population 50) where the hotel is located. When his father who owned a small bar died, Signore Beppe took over - although he was only a boy at the time. The rest is history: the bar grew into a restaurant, the restaurant into a tiny hotel, the small hotel into a delightful resort. Such a success story is not surprising when you meet Signore Beppe. He speaks no English. He does not need to. His charismatic charm transcends all language barriers. It is no wonder his restaurant - isolated in the countryside - is filled each night with chicly dressed Italian clientele: Beppe greets each of them with an exuberant warmth, and the food is outstanding, truly a gourmet delight. Since we originally visited the Locanda del Sant'Uffizio, Beppe and his wife have been joined in the operation of the Locanda del Sant'Uffizio by their two sons: Fabio, a chemical engineer, collaborates with the chef and Massimo, an architect, assists his father in the welcoming of guests. Happily for the visitors from abroad, both sons speak English and French.

LOCANDA DEL SANT'UFFIZIO
RISTORANTE DA BEPPE
Owner: Giuseppe Firato
Near Moncalvo
14030 Cioccaro di Penango, Italy
tel: (0141) 91271 fax: (0141) 916068
35 rooms: Lire 440,000
Rate includes breakfast & dinner
Hotel closed January & August 10-20
Restaurant closed Tuesdays
Credit cards: MC VS
5 km SE of Moncalvo, 60 km E of Turin
21 km N of Asti toward Moncalvo

The Hotel Menardi dates back 200 years.   Originally it was a peasant's farmhouse, but as Cortina's popularity as a fabulous ski center has spread so has the town, and now the farm is located right on the outskirts of town on the main road heading north.   Nevertheless, the Menardi family, who have owned the home for a century and a half, have managed to maintain the country flavor through the use of many antiques, marvelous old prints on the walls, old clocks, giant dowry chests, Oriental carpets, and beautiful hanging cupboards - all set off by the warmth and gaiety of flowers everywhere.   The bedrooms vary in decor but are all pleasant and with private bath.   In addition to the original inn which has 40 rooms, there is a new house with an additional 15 rooms.   It seems that, due to its location on the main road, the Menardi farm just naturally evolved into a hotel.   At first it gave shelter to the men carting loads over the Cimabanche Pass who needed a place to sleep - more often than not in the hay loft.   Today the inn is a simple, but wonderful, small hotel whose special ingredient is the old-fashioned warmth and hospitality of the gracious Menardis.

HOTEL MENARDI
Owner: Menardi Family
112 Via Majon
32043 Cortina D'Ampezzo, Italy
tel: (0436) 2400   fax: (0436) 862183
55 rooms: Lire 190,000-320,000
Rate includes breakfast & dinner
Open July-September, late December-March
Credit cards: VS
Old farmhouse, many antiques
133 km E of Bolzano
71 km N of Belluno

You would never "happen upon" the Residenza S. Andrea al Farinaio because it is truly located off the beaten path (in fact you really must write or call ahead for detailed instructions if you ever hope to find it), but once you have settled in, the location is really quite convenient, especially if you want a home base for exploring both Tuscany and Umbria.   And, for those looking for a well-priced place to stay without sacrificing comfort, the Residenza S. Andrea al Farinaio might be the perfect solution.   The oldest part of the inn dates back to the 13th Century when it was the home for the priests tending a church which stood across the road.   The present owner, Patrizia Nappi, is a warm and gracious hostess, speaks excellent English, and has lovingly transformed the old stone house into a cozy inn, combining some modern pictures, furniture and knickknacks with lovely antiques. Of the five bedrooms, three have private baths.   My favorite is the large guest room at the top of the steps.   The most wonderful room in the house is the dining room with its massive darkened wooden beams, large open fireplace, beautiful antique trestle table, colorful plates adorning the walls, and lots of copper pots and pans.   If you make arrangements in advance, you can have the pleasure of dining here family-style with other guests.   This is one of the highlights of staying at the Residenza: enjoying a simple, yet superb meal at the long, handsome table adorned with fresh flowers and glowing candles, and in front of a crackling fire.

RESIDENZA S. ANDREA AL FARINAIO
Owner: Patrizia Nappi
San Andrea al Farinaio, 118
52040 Terontola di Cortona, Italy
tel: (0575) 677736
5 rooms: Lire 130,000
Open all year
Credit cards: none accepted
75 km E of Siena, 10 km SE of Cortona

Hotel Descriptions

Corvara, a mountain village in northeastern Italy, is popular with guests who enjoy walking through high alpine meadows in summer and skiing down snow covered slopes in winter. Although the Dolomite region is one of the most beautiful in Italy and offers many hotels, there is not a rich choice for visitors who prefer small inns with an old-world, antique ambiance. Luckily, La Perla, located in the center of Corvara, offers not only a convenient place to stay, but also a cozy ambiance. This small inn is owned and managed by the Costa family who lovingly oversee every detail. The day I visited, Mrs. Costa was busily engaged in supervising the table arrangements to be sure everything was perfect. One enters into a large reception lobby where heavy wooden beams, Oriental carpets on tiled floors, fresh plants and country-patterned drapes set the mood. But the real winners are the dining rooms. There are a series of lovely places to eat: each with its own personality - all absolutely oozing with cozy charm. Antique clocks, tiled ovens, low beamed ceilings, painted chests, warm antique wood paneling, abundant accents of copper plus handsome linens, fresh flowers and candlelight make each room a dream. The guest rooms have all the modern amenities, but do not display the old-world ambiance of the public rooms.

LA PERLA
Owner: Costa Family
39033 Corvara, Italy
tel: (0471) 836132 fax: (0471) 836568
50 rooms: Lire 180,000-320,000
Open Jul 1-Sep 20 & Dec 16-Apr 25
Credit cards: DC VS
Swimming pool
65 km E of Bolzano, 47 km W of Cortina
U.S. Rep: Romantik Hotels
Rep tel: 800-826-0015

The 19th-century Castello di Pomerio dates from the 9th Century and has been renovated with exquisite taste and quality. As you roam the antique-filled rooms, you will be aware of the impact of their perfection. Each detail of restoration shows loving care: in fact, even ancient frescos have been meticulously restored. Some of the bedrooms are in the main castle and others are in a wing across the road that is cleverly connected to the castle by a tunnel so that you still feel a part of the main hotel. All of the bedrooms vary in decor, but all are outstanding. Most of the ones I saw had wonderful wooden beds and attractive heavy curtains; many had cozy fireplaces - all had charm. For the exercise enthusiast, there is a tennis court plus both an indoor and an outdoor swimming pool. Through the ages, this hotel has changed hands many times. At one point, its past even included use as a silk factory. How lucky for the tourist that now the building houses such a romantic hotel where one can stop for a few days and live like a king in his "own" castle.

HOTEL CASTELLO DI POMERIO
Owner: Set Hotels
Via Como, 5
22036 Pomerio di Erba, Italy
tel: (031) 627516 fax: (031) 628245
54 rooms: Lire 250,000-350,000
Open all year
Credit cards: all major
Sauna, inside & outside pools, tennis court
Near Lake Como
44 km N of Milan
14 km E of Como

The Punta Est is a lovely old villa perched on a hilltop overlooking the sea. When the home was converted to a villa an annex was added to provide more bedrooms. However, it still gives the friendly feeling of a private home. This warmth of reception and attention to detail are the result of the management of the Podesta family who own and manage the inn. They seem dedicated to making your stay as enjoyable as possible - even their German Shepherd seems to want to welcome you. There are little terraces with lovely views snuggled at various levels among the trees and on one of these terraces is a swimming pool. There is also access to the public beach of Finale Ligure which can easily be reached by walking down the path to the main highway and following the tunnel beneath the highway to the beach. The rooms in the main villa are smaller and more old-fashioned than those in the newer annex which are more reminiscent of an American motel. There is a small dining room for breakfast which is especially inviting with its blue and white English bone china service. This is just one example of a very nice touch offered by owners who really want to please.

HOTEL PUNTA EST
Owner: Podesta Family
17024 Finale Ligure, Italy
tel: (019) 600611 fax: (019) 600611
37 rooms: Lire 220,000-240,000
Suite Lire 340,000
3 day minimum stay requirement
Open May to October
Credit cards: AX VS
Pool and access to the beach
Italian Riviera
72 km SW of Genoa, 75 km E of San Remo

The Grand Hotel Villa Cora is a mansion, originally built during the 19th Century by the Baron Oppenheim as a gift for his beautiful young bride.   Among the many romantic tales of the Villa Cora is the one about Oppenheim's wife who, so the story goes, became enamored of one of her many admirers.   The jealous baron was so enraged that he threatened to burn the entire mansion.   Luckily for you and me, he was stopped in time from this mad endeavor by his friends, and today this magnificent villa is a stunning hotel.   Although only about a 5-minute taxi ride from the center of Florence (or a 15-minute walk), the Grand Hotel Villa Cora is eons away in atmosphere.   You feel more like a guest on a country estate rather than in a city hotel.   The villa is set in intricate gardens and even has a pool.   The interior of the hotel is rather ornate and sumptuous.   You can almost hear the sounds of laughter and music drifting through the gardens, and indeed the mansion has always been famous for its dramatic parties: at one time the villa was the residence of Napoleon's wife, Empress Eugenia, whose gay entertaining was the talk of Florence.   Now this grand palace-like home can be yours for days of dreams and romance.   Note: there is free limousine service for guests to and from Florence.

GRAND HOTEL VILLA CORA
Manager: Valerio Rastrelli
Viale Machiavelli, 18/20
50125 Florence, Italy
tel: (055) 2298451 fax: (055) 229086
48 rooms: Lire 587,000
Open all year
Credit cards: all major
Sumptuous villa - park like setting
Swimming pool, restaurant, piano bar
15-minute walk from heart of Florence

After being closed for two years for complete renovation, the Hotel Helvetia & Bristol reopened in late 1989 and instantly became, in my estimation, the finest luxury hotel in the center of Florence. Nothing has been spared to make this show-place a true beauty. The decor is outstanding. The lounges, exquisitely decorated with an elegant, yet extremely comfortable, home-like ambiance, exude quality without flamboyance. Each of the guest rooms is also superbly decorated, and, as in a private home, no two are alike. Abundant use of exquisite padded fabric wall coverings, with color-coordinated draperies, upholstered chairs and bed-spreads along with lovely antiques makes each one special. I fell in love with each of the rooms, but my *very favorites* were mini suites: room 257 in gorgeous shades of muted green and room 363 in lovely golds, creams, and dusty pinks, sumptuous marble bathroom with jacuzzi tub, heated towel racks, enormous towels, plus the added bonus of a tiny terrace. The dining room, cozy yet elegant with dark walls and soft lighting, specializes in Tuscan cuisine. For light refreshments, a cool drink or just relaxing, the "Giardino d'Inverno" (Winter Garden) is a marvelous retreat - light and airy with a domed, old-fashioned skylight, potted plants and nostalgic wicker furniture. The Helvetia & Bristol is expensive, but no more so than the other luxury hotels in Florence, and for those who appreciate quality and refinement, it is unsurpassed.

HOTEL HELVETIA & BRISTOL
Director: Franco Ensoli
Via dei Pescioni, 2
50123 Florence, Italy
tel: (055) 287814 fax: (055) 288353
50 rooms: Lire 457,000-552,000
Credit cards: all major
Luxurious hotel with finest decor
In the heart of Florence

Each time we visit the Loggiato dei Serviti, we are again impressed with what a pleasant small hotel this is for the money. Many of the hotels in Florence are lovely, but fabulously expensive: others are reasonably priced, but shabby and dark. So it is an exceedingly happy surprise to find a light, airy, antique-filled small hotel - at a reasonable rate. This is not a deluxe hotel, but we think you will be well pleased. The building dates back to the 16th Century when it was built for the order of the "Serviti" fathers. The character of the original building has been meticulously maintained adding greatly to the charm of the hotel. The location is superb: right in the heart of Florence on the historical Piazza SS. Annunziata. There is a small reception area as you enter, beyond which is an intimate little bar where snacks are served (there is no restaurant at the hotel). A miniature elevator - just large enough for two people to squeeze into - takes you upstairs to the spacious bedrooms, each with private bath and each individually decorated in excellent taste with liberal use of antiques. There are four suites, one of which even has two bedrooms and two bathrooms. Although of course more expensive than the standard double room, these suites are most attractive and a good value for a family.

LOGGIATO DEI SERVITI
Owner: Budini Gattai
Piazza SS. Annunziata, 3
50122 Florence, Italy
tel: (055) 219165 fax: (055) 289595
29 rooms: Lire 165,500
4 suites: Lire 200,000-400,000
Open all year
Credit cards: all major
Antique-filled small hotel, no restaurant
In the heart of Florence

The Lungarno Hotel is superbly located directly on the Arno River and only a few minutes' walk from the Ponte Vecchio. Although most of the hotel is of new construction, the architect cleverly incorporated an ancient stone tower into the hotel so it is easy to rationalize including this hotel - one of my favorites in Florence - into this travel guide. The interior of the hotel is traditional rather than antique in decor, but the decorating is done with excellent taste and the effect is most pleasing. Lovely soft colors are used throughout with beautiful prints on the wall and many fresh flowers. The bedrooms are very comfortable and those who book well in advance can request one of the rooms overlooking the Arno. Those who really plan ahead might even be lucky enough to secure one of the few rooms with a balcony overlooking the river. What a treat to sit on your own little balcony in the evening and watch the Arno fade into gold and the Ponte Vecchio glow in the setting sun. There are several rooms in the tower itself, one of which is especially romantic with its remaining old stone wall and its staircase that leads up to a little balcony and a third bed. Several of the other rooms in the new portion of the hotel also have lofts which can be used as sleeping alcoves.

LUNGARNO HOTEL
Manager: Nedo Naldini
Borgo San Jacopo, 14
50125 Florence, Italy
tel: (055) 264211 fax: (055) 268437
66 rooms: Lire 297,000
Open all year
Credit cards: all major
Some rooms with view terraces
Short walk to Ponte Vecchio
Directly on the Arno River

Mario's came highly recommended to us by several readers, and after seeing the hotel for ourselves, we agree that it is a delightful small hotel, moderately priced for Florence. It is conveniently located two blocks from the train station, and within easy walking distance to the city's major sightseeing. From the street, the appeal of the hotel is not readily evident as it is housed in a rather nondescript building, but after ascending the stairs to the second floor and stepping into the cozy, beamed-ceilinged lobby, you know you've arrived at a well-tended small hotel with an old Florentine ambiance. Facing the reception desk is an inviting sitting area with sofas arranged under a wall of pictures, Persian carpets enhancing the dark tile floors, and artfully arranged pictures and plants setting off the cream colored walls. Each of the guest rooms has a country fresh feeling with antique armoires, wrought iron headboards, rustic wooden desk and chairs and pretty bedspreads. The rooms are not large, but are very pleasing and immaculately tidy. A copious breakfast is served family-style at long dining tables in a charming room whose walls are hung with many pictures. Guests choose from a wonderful selection of breads, cheese, cereal, boiled eggs, coffee, tea, and chocolate. The nicest aspect of this hotel is the fact that it is small enough to be very personalized and Mario sees to it that every guest feels special.

MARIO'S
Owner: Mario Noce
Via Faenza, 89
50123 Florence, Italy
tel: (055) 216801 fax: (055) 212039
16 rooms: Lire 120,000-155,000
Open all year
Credit cards: all major
No restaurant in hotel but many nearby
2 blocks from train station in Florence

The Monna Lisa, located about a five-minute walk from the heart of Florence, is a real gem. Facing directly onto a small side street, the simple exterior gives no hint of the appealing small hotel secreted behind the heavy doors. The present owners, the Ciardi-Dupre family, are direct descendants of the very famous sculptor, Giovanni Dupre. This heritage undoubtedly accounts for the many art treasures found accenting every nook and cranny of this little inn. Many elegant, family heirloom antiques are also displayed throughout the Monna Lisa. The hotel has only 20 rooms, which are always occupied. They vary in size and decor - some with handsome antique beds and massive beamed ceilings. A few have balconies overlooking the lovely back garden. The exceptional appeal of the hotel, however, is not the guest rooms, but the public areas: the beautiful lounge, cozy bar, small parlor and spacious reception area from which a dramatic stone staircase gracefully sweeps up to the second floor guest rooms. The Monna Lisa is very home-like; in warm weather guests usually relax in the secluded back garden. Another real bonus if you are arriving by car: to the rear of the property is a parking area. The Monna Lisa was originally an elegant Renaissance palace and you will certainly feel like nobility while a guest at this hotel.

HOTEL MONNA LISA
Owner: Ciardi-Dupre Family
Manager: Riccardo Sardei
Borgo Pinti, 27
50121 Florence, Italy
tel: (055) 2479751 fax: (055) 2479755
20 rooms: Lire 210,000-300,000
Open all year
Credit cards: all major
Exceptionally delightful small inn
5-minute walk from heart of Florence

The Regency is located on a small park-like square only a ten-minute walk from the heart of Florence. It is, however, a world away in atmosphere - instead of the noise of motorcycles and the bustle of tourist-filled streets, you have a peaceful, quiet, elegant setting. The mood of being "away from it all" is enhanced as you enter the hotel. Again you are protected: the front door is usually kept locked and only guests of the hotel are allowed inside. You ring the front door bell just as you would in a private home. Although small, the Regency is a deluxe hotel and, in fact, it is quite amazing that with only 38 rooms the Regency can offer so many of the luxuries that are usually found only in larger hotels, such as a concierge to assist you with any of your personal needs and an intimate restaurant in a gorgeous wood paneled dining room. A larger restaurant will soon be open in an adjoining townhouse. The bedrooms are spacious and luxurious, with excellent lighting and elegant bathrooms. I would prefer a few more antiques, but these are found mostly in the lounges and the dining room. At the present time, the Regency spreads into several adjacent "homes" with a garden connecting the wings.

HOTEL REGENCY
Owner: Amedeo Ottaviani
Manager: Pietro Panelli
Piazza Massimo d'Azeglio, 3
50121 Florence, Italy
tel: (055) 245247 fax: (055) 2342938
38 rooms: Lire 510,000-561,000
Open all year
Credit cards: all major
Quiet, elegant, "home-like" hotel
10-minute walk to heart of Florence
U.S. Rep: LHW
Rep tel: 800-223-6800

For years I have heard about the charms of the Hotel Tornabuoni Beacci.   In fact, on previous trips to Florence I tried to see the hotel, but the rooms were always completely occupied (as they usually are) and there was no one available to show me around.   This time, in spite of it being a very busy season, I was able to take the "grand tour".   It was worth waiting for.   For those who want an excellent value in the heart of Florence, the Hotel Tornabuoni Beacci is quite special.   The owner, Signora Beacci, manages the hotel and is ever-present.   She cares about every detail of the operation, running this small hotel like she would her own home.   An indeed, the appearance is like a family home, with cherished antiques creating a cozy ambiance in all the public rooms and also accenting the furnishings in the bedrooms.   From the outside, one would never guess at the oasis within.   Only a discreet sign alerts passersby that there is a hotel on the third floor of this nondescript building in the heart of the city.   After entering a somewhat dismal lobby, a tiny elevator slowly rises to the third floor reception desk and the hallway which leads into the hotel.   One of the nicest features of this little inn is its roof garden where, surrounded by fragrant flowers, tables are set up for guests to relax and enjoy a superb view over the rooftops of Florence.

HOTEL TORNABUONI BEACCI
Owner: Mrs. Lensi Orlandi Beacci
Via Tornabuoni, 3
50123 Florence, Italy
tel: (055) 212645 or (055) 283594
30 rooms: Lire 220,000-250,000
Open all year
Credit cards: all major
Marvelous roof garden - charming views
In the center of Florence

Florence is probably one of Italy's most romantic cities: Torre di Bellosguardo is definitely one of Italy's most romantic hotels. What a jewel. This is such a special inn that we are almost reluctant to share the secret. The Torre di Bellosguardo is housed in a sensational villa nestled on the shelf of a hill with a panoramic view of Florence - the tiled rooftops, steeples, towers and domes seem like a fairyland at your fingertips. I thought nothing could be more spectacular than when the setting sun painted Florence in a rosy glow at sunset. But then the twilight faded into darkness and the lights of the city seemed to dance below the starry sky and I decided this was almost more spectacular. It is not surprising the setting of the Torre di Bellosguardo is so fabulous. It was chosen by a nobleman, Guido Cavalcanti (a friend of Dante's) as the most beautiful site in Florence to build his villa. The villa is owned today by Amerigo Franchetti who inherited the fabulous property from his grandmother, a baroness. Each room is a treasure decorated with marvelous antiques. The garden is a meticulously groomed delight and highlights a splendid pool on the terrace overlooking Florence. Staying here is certainly like being the pampered guest of nobility: which of course you really are. The best surprise of all is the price. Though only a very short drive to the heart of Florence, the cost is much less than staying in the center of the city at a deluxe hotel ... and more romantic.

TORRE DI BELLOSGUARDO
Owner: Amerigo Franchetti
Via Roti Michelozzi, 2
50124 Florence, Italy
tel: (055) 229529 fax: (055) 229008
16 rooms: Lire 380,000, Suites to Lire 570,000
Open all year
Credit cards: all major
5-minute drive to heart of Florence

As an alternative to staying in downtown Florence, you might want to consider instead the Villa La Massa which is located on the banks of the Arno about a 15-minute drive from town. The Villa La Massa is actually composed of three buildings - each old and each having its own unique charm. This beautiful estate originally belonged to the rich and powerful Giraldi family: inscribed tombstones, underground tunnels and a chapel still remain from this period of the villa's ancient history. Although the Villa La Massa is very old, the hotel offers all of the modern amenities including tennis courts, a swimming pool, air conditioning, refrigerators in the guest rooms. The restaurant, *Il Verrocchio*, has a beautiful terrace for outdoor dining overlooking the Arno river and offers the best of Tuscan specialties. If you have a car, then the Villa La Massa might make an appealing alternative to staying in the heart of Florence: especially in summer when you can do your sightseeing during the day and return to a pool and garden setting at night.

HOTEL VILLA LA MASSA
Owner: Carlo Grillini
50010 Candeli
Florence, Italy
tel: (055) 632579 fax: (055) 666141
40 rooms: Lire 320,000-490,000
Open all year
Credit cards: all major
Swimming pool, tennis courts
Located on bend of Arno River
7 km E of Florence

The Bencista is a real "find" for the traveller looking for a congenial, appealing, family run hotel near Florence which has charm and yet is reasonably priced. This delightful old villa, romantically nestled in the foothills overlooking Florence, is owned and managed by the Simoni family who are always about, personally seeing to every need of their guests. Simone Simoni speaks excellent English, and on the day of my arrival he was patiently engrossed in conversation with one of the guests, giving him tips for sightseeing. Downstairs there are a jumble of rooms, each nicely decorated with rather dark, Victorian furniture. Upstairs are the bedrooms which vary in size, location, and furnishings. Some are far superior to others; however, they are all divided into only two price categories: with or without private bathroom. Many people return year after year to "their own" favorite room. During the season, reservations are usually given only to guests who plan to spend several days at the hotel - this is an easy requirement because the hotel is beautifully located for sightseeing in both Florence and Tuscany. (If you do not have a car, there is a bus at the top of the road which runs regularly into Florence.) Two meals (breakfast and a choice of lunch or dinner of family-style Italian cooking) are included in the price. One of the outstanding features of the pensione is its splendid terrace where guests can enjoy a sweeping panorama of Florence.

PENSIONE BENCISTA
Owner: Simone Simoni
50014 Fiesole (Florence), Italy
tel: (055) 59163 fax: (055) 59163
43 rooms: Lire 148,000-192,000
Rate includes breakfast & dinner
Open all year
Credit cards: none accepted
8 km NE of Florence

It would be difficult to find another hotel with as many attributes as the Villa San Michele.   In fact, almost impossible.   How could one surpass a wooded hillside setting overlooking Florence, a stunning view, gorgeous antiques, impeccable management, gourmet dining, and, as if this were not enough, a building designed by Michelangelo.   The Villa San Michele was originally a monastery whose inner courtyard dates back to the 15th Century.   No expense has been spared in the reconstruction of this fabulous building to maintain the ancient ambiance.   There are only 28 guest rooms, and, although not large, they are decorated with elegant taste.   The lounges, dining rooms, terraces and gardens are also exquisite. Breakfast and either dinner or lunch are compulsory, but this is no problem since the food is delicious.   Meals can be enjoyed either in a beautiful dining room or on a lovely veranda which stretches along the entire length of the building.   A swimming pool has been built on a secluded little terrace above the hotel, and, as with every feature of the Villa San Michele, it is beautiful, perfectly situated to capture the view and surrounded by fragrant gardens.

VILLA SAN MICHELE
Manager: Maurizio Saccani
Via Doccia, 4, Fiesole
50014 Florence, Italy
tel: (055) 59451 fax: (055) 598734
28 rooms: Lire 1,27,6000-1,958,000
Rates include breakfast & dinner
Open April to December
Credit cards: all major
Pool, luxury hotel in hills above Florence
7 km NE of Florence
U.S. Rep: LHW 800-223-6800

The Hotel Villa del Sogno is perched on a hillside across the road from, and overlooking beautiful Lake Garda. I am not sure of the history of the villa, but apparently it was an estate - obviously of a family of means, for the hotel is a prime piece of property. A small private road winds up the hill through a grove of trees until the villa is spotted, a traditional ochre-colored, red-tiled-roof building set off with white trim and green shutters. As you enter the hotel, it is as if you were in a private home. A large wooden, open staircase leads to the upper floors where the spacious bedrooms are attractively decorated in traditional style furniture. The choice rooms of course are those in the front with a view of the lake. One of the very finest features of the Villa del Sogno is its especially large terrace in the back of the hotel which has a majestic view out over the trees to the lake. The day I visited, many of the guests were enjoying afternoon tea (the hotel seems to cater to small British tour groups) as they savored the view from the comfort of lounge chairs. Another favorite retreat is the swimming pool which is tucked onto a terrace nestled to the side of the hotel. The grounds surrounding the pool are quite lovely, with potted plants placed strategically about the various levels of park like grounds.

VILLA DEL SOGNO
Owner: Aldo Calderan
25083 Fasano di Gardone Riviera, Italy
tel: (0365) 290181 fax: (0365) 290230
35 rooms: Lire 240,000-280,000
Open April to mid-October
Credit cards: all major
Minimum stay 3 days
Lake views, swimming pool, tennis
2 km NE of Gardone Riviera
130 km E of Milan, 68 km W of Verona

I was enchanted with the Villa Fiordaliso (a fetching pink and white villa superbly located on the shore of Lake Garda) when I spent the night in one of its antique-filled bedrooms overlooking the lake several years ago.   At that time, I wrote a glowing description of this beautiful little hotel, only to learn from the manager that I was one of the last guests - the villa was closing to the public.   Nevertheless, when researching for a later edition, I went by the Villa Fiordaliso "for old times' sake" and, to my delight, found it open again as a small inn.   Although the emphasis now is definitely on dining (the meals are expensive, but excellent), there are seven bedrooms - each unique in decor, yet each with every modern comfort.   The rooms facing the lake have a lovely view, and are quieter since they are away from the noise of the street.   Throughout the interior there is a blend of antique and modern furniture, nicely set off by inlaid parquet flooring, engraved golden ceilings, marbles and alabasters.   For history buffs, the villa offers a bit of romance - the Villa Fiordaliso was a gift of Mussolini to his mistress, Claretta Petacci.   In fact, Claretta's own bedroom is one of the rooms available and is a real winner with an enormous marble bathroom.

VILLA FIORDALISO
Owner: Pierantonio Ambrosi
Manager: Stefano Sganzerla
Via Zanardelli, 132
25083 Gardone Riviera, Italy
tel: (0365) 20158 fax: (0365) 290011
7 rooms: Lire 350,000
    (Claretta's suite 600,000)
Rates include breakfast & dinner
Open March through December
Credit cards: all major
130 km E of Milan, 66 km W of Verona

When we first saw the Hotel Villa Giulia it was rated by the government as a third class pensione.   However, the hotel is no longer a simple pensione.   On our last visit we were pleased to note that all the rooms now have a private bathroom and even a swimming pool has been built into the garden.   The inn is a Victorian-style villa in a large park which extends down to Lake Garda.   A dramatic staircase at the end of the hallway leads to the simple bedrooms.   In addition to the rooms in the main villa, guest rooms are available in a modern annex.   On the same level as the entrance hall is a dining room which is quite appealing with enormous chandeliers and antique-style chairs.   On a lower level, opening out onto the garden, is another dining room which is quite modern and lacking in charm.   When the weather is warm, the favorite place to dine is on the terrace where tables are set to enjoy the sun and a view of the lake.   Wherever you choose to dine, you will enjoy good home-style Italian cooking - it is not surprising that the food is well prepared since Signora Bombardelli, the owner, is usually bustling about in the kitchen personally overseeing the preparation of the next meal.   She does not speak much English, but is extremely gracious and is always about seeing that her guests are happy.   Not fancy, the Hotel Villa Giulia offers a very pleasant stay at reasonable prices with a superb lakefront location.

HOTEL VILLA GIULIA
Owner: Bombardelli Family
Via Rimembranza, 20
25084 Gargnano, Lake Garda, Italy
tel: (0365) 71289 fax: (0365) 72774
30 rooms: Lire 130,000 (3 day minimum)
Open April to October
Credit cards: all major
Swimming pool, sauna
140 km E of Milan, 78 km W of Verona

We first discovered Baia d'Oro when we stopped for a cup of coffee in the small lakeside village of Villa Gargnano and saw a lakefront terrace, complete with jaunty, gay umbrellas.   Walking over to investigate, we found fronting the pretty terrace a tiny bar, a lounge with lots of copper on the walls, and a dining room whose doors opened out onto the sun-filled deck extending over the lake which we had been admiring from a distance.   Owned by the Terzi family, the Baia d'Oro exhibits the charm and special character that are the imprint of a caring, very personal management.   Although not a fancy hotel by any means, this little inn has a wealth of attributes frequently not found in larger hotels of much higher rating. Except when the weather is chilly, all the meals are served outside on the lovely deck stretching over the lake.   The beautifully presented food is delicious and the menu extensive, specializing in fresh fish.   An added bonus while you dine is to watch the motor boats pull next to the dock, tie up, and unload their cargo of happy, hungry customers.   The bedrooms are extremely basic in furnishings, but they all have private bathrooms.   Even though the decor is dated, the rooms overlooking the lake are romantic - definitely for the young at heart.   The walls of this homey inn are adorned with the paintings of owner Gianbattista Terzi, a well-known artist in Europe, whose works also hang in many galleries.

BAIA D'ORO
Owner: Terzi Family
Via Liberta
25085 Gargnano-Villa, Italy
tel: (0365) 71171 fax: (0365) 72568
13 rooms: Lire 240,000 (with breakfast & dinner)
Open April through October
Credit cards: all major
Located directly on Lake Garda
140 km E of Milan, 78 km W of Verona

Finally there is a very special place to stay near the Rome airport.   However, to merely say that a void has been filled is totally inadequate for La Posta Vecchia without a doubt offers some of the most sensational accommodations in all of Italy ... in all the world.   Not that everyone will be able to afford to stay here for this is an expensive small inn - very expensive, but if you have the money, it is a real bargain.   For this is the opportunity of a lifetime for those who want to taste the life-style of the rich and famous.   La Posta Vecchia was the home of the late John Paul Getty, his Italian villa nestled on the edge of the ocean just north of the Rome airport.   Just imagine: there are only ten rooms, mostly suites, tucked into an enormous mansion, secluded by manicured gardens artfully created to emphasize the ruins of a Pompeii-like Roman villa whose beautiful mosaic floor peeks from between surrounding flowers and hedges.   Within the villa, priceless antique furniture, statues, and fabulous fabrics adorn the rooms, artfully blended by Getty's interior designer to create an opulent, tasteful splendor.   For Getty, nothing was too special, nothing too expensive.   All has been retained as it was in Getty's day, the only changes being some cosmetic spiffing such as painting and new drapes (this was taking awhile because the factory in Paris where the original fabric had been woven had to be tracked down - but replacements were on the way at the time of our visit).   The new owner has accomplished a remarkable feat of returning the villa to its original magnificence.   The primary use of the villa is for small groups that book the entire hotel for private conferences, think tanks, seminars, and family reunions.   If you want the entire villa for an exclusive holiday, you need have no worry about security since columns, discreetly positioned on each corner of the property, send out detector rays to keep anyone from the premises, plus of course bullet proof glass in the Getty bedroom and steel infrastructure in the walls.   Also, should you want to bring your staff, the third floor is well equipped for your maids and butlers.

When Getty was renovating the villa for his personal use and installing the magnificent pool in the northern wing of the house, he found the villa dated back much earlier than he originally speculated. Beneath the house were the foundations of a Roman villa thought perhaps to be the weekend retreat of Julius Caesar. Getty, whom you know was profoundly interested in archaeology, spared no expense to preserve this antiquity. The Roman ruins now encompass the lower level of the home and guests can wonder at the gorgeous mosaic floors, walls and pottery displayed like in a living museum. Parts of the museum can be viewed from the upper level where a panel of glass has been installed in the floor so the mosaic under-flooring can be viewed. There is even a workshop in this subterranean museum, where archaeologists under the supervision of the Department of Fine Arts continue to piece together the puzzle of this fascinating villa. Note: Since La Posta Vecchia is ideally suited for small groups - such as an exclusive house party or summit meeting of heads of state - there will be times when the entire villa is rented and rooms won't be available for individual bookings. But, if you are lucky and can snare a room, this is truly an experience of a lifetime.

LA POSTA VECCHIA
Manager: Mario Ciorciolini
00055 Palo Laziale, Ladispoli, Italy
tel: (06) 9949500 fax: (06) 9949507
10 rooms: Lire 700,000 minimum
 Getty's suite: Lire 2,000,000
 Lunch or dinner: Lire 120,000 per person
Credit cards: all major
Sensational home of J. Paul Getty
Private beach, swimming pool
Private small museum
2 km S of Ladispoli at Palo, private road
35 km N of Rome Airport, Ocean-front

The Villa La Principessa is a stately, traditional country mansion surrounded by beautiful gardens.   In a park-like setting behind the hotel is a large swimming pool with lounge chairs and umbrellas invitingly set for guests to relax and enjoy the sun. In the distance are lush, green hills.   The entire effect is refreshing and serene. The interior of the villa does not maintain the same degree of quiet elegance as does the exterior: the entry hall has some fine antiques and a beautifully paneled ceiling, but the carpet is a loud plaid which would be better suited for a Scottish castle and in one of the lounge rooms, the carpet is purple and the walls and draperies a bright green.   The dining room, however, tones down with more muted colors and is quite attractive.   The Villa La principessa is located between the popular tourist destinations of Lucca and Pisa.   As there are no deluxe places to stay in either Lucca nor Pisa, the Villa La Principessa makes an excellent choice for those seeking well-maintained, luxury accommodations in a resort-like setting.

HOTEL VILLA LA PRINCIPESSA
Manager: Giancarlo Mugnani
55050 Massa Pisana
Lucca, Italy
tel: (0583) 370037 fax: (0583) 379019
44 rooms: Lire 396,000-451,000
Closed January & February
Credit cards: all major
4 km S of Lucca on old road to Pisa
18 km N of Pisa

The Albergo del Sole, located about an hour's drive south of Milan, came highly recommended to us as one of Italy's finest "restaurants with rooms" so we arrived eagerly for our first visit. Happily, this little inn surpassed our highest expectations, offering an elegantly rustic setting and delicious meals. This 600 year old farmhouse is now a food connoisseur's dream come true. From the moment you enter this old stone home you are enveloped in a country ambiance enhanced by fine antiques, heavy beams, copper pots hanging on the walls and extravagant bouquets of flowers. The heart of the inn is its kitchen, long famous as one of Italy's finest, and well-deserving of its Michelin star. The food, featuring regional specialties prepared from the freshest of locally produced ingredients, is very expensive, but outstanding. If you cannot overnight here, the inn is still worth a visit simply for its atmosphere and cuisine. However, if possible, plan to spend the night so you can linger over your dinner and savor the fine food and wines. Some of the guest rooms are in the main building, others are in rooms tucked around the back garden. Each of the bedrooms is nicely decorated, but with a much more modern mood than the dining rooms. Although the food and country style furnishings are outstanding, it is the traditional Italian welcome and caring warmth of the owners, Silvana and Franco Colombani, that make the Albergo del Sole so special. Note: very little English spoken.

ALBERGO DEL SOLE
Owners: Silvana & Franco Colombani
Via Trabattoni 22
20076 Maleo, Italy
tel: (0377) 58142 fax: (0377) 458058
7 rooms: Lire 272,000-320,000
Closed January and August
Credit cards: AX VS
60 km S of Milan, 23 km W of Cremona

The Hotel Santavenere was a wonderful surprise. I had seen pictures of the hotel before I arrived and it looked rather like a motel - a long, narrow building with each floor a row of guest rooms. The photographs did not do it justice - the hotel is absolutely a knockout. From the moment you walk into the lobby, the gracious ambiance of an exquisite country home surrounds you. The living room is elegant, but not "stuffy" - soft, comfortable sofas and lounge chairs slipcovered in an attractive country print form cozy conversation nooks. Excellent antiques lend further charm. Plus, there are many nautical accents, such as models of sailboats, giving even more interest to the room. The dining room follows in excellent taste - a large, airy room with highbacked wooden chairs, fresh flowers on the tables, and white linen cloths. The bedrooms are beautifully decorated with excellent copies of antiques and have modern bathrooms. Each bedroom opens onto its own terrace or balcony with lovely sea views. The location too is exceptional: there is a beautiful green lawn adorned with a swimming pool which stretches to the side of the hotel. Beyond the lawn the cliffs drop down a steep wooded hillside to the sea and a small private pier.

HOTEL SANTAVENERE
85040 Maratea, Italy
Localita Fiumicello
tel: (0973) 876910 fax: (0973) 876985
44 rooms: Lire 584,000-738,000
Rates include breakfast, lunch & dinner
Open June to September 26
Credit cards: VS AX DC
On the sea, pool, tennis
220 km S of Naples, 5 km W of Maratea

Once in a while a hotel is so perfect that it is tempting not to include it - selfishly fearful that if everyone knows how exceptional it is there might not be "room in the inn" when we return. The Castel Freiberg is just that special, but conscience dictates sharing with you our Shangri-La. This fantasy castle cresting a hilltop in the mountains near Merano exudes charm. All of the public rooms are a decorator's dream where priceless antiques abound. The bedrooms, each individual in decor, are all tastefully furnished and some have balconies overlooking the mountains. Even if the setting were not perfect, this castle would be a "winner" because of its enchanting decor, but add to this a gorgeous restaurant in a richly paneled room with gourmet cooking, and what else could you possibly desire? Well, there is more. If you talk to the masterful and professional concierge, you will find that surrounding the Castel Freiberg is a maze of splendid walking paths. Also, of course, there is a beautiful pool in a garden setting with the mountains as a dramatic backdrop, as well as an inside pool, clay tennis courts, an exercise room, and more - you must go to see for yourself.

HOTEL CASTEL FREIBERG
Owner: Bortolotti Family
39012 Merano, Italy
tel: (0473) 244196 fax: (0473) 244488
35 rooms: Lire 297,000-319,000
Open April 22 to November
Credit cards: all major
2 pools, tennis, grounds
In the countryside 7 km S of Merano
28 km NW of Bolzano
U.S. Rep: David B. Mitchell
Rep tel: 800-372-1323

Schloss Labers is a lovely old castle which dates back to the 11th Century. It has a picturesque setting on a hillside surrounded by vineyards and overlooking the beautiful Merano Valley which is framed by dramatic mountains. Although not luxurious, this castle has character and charm. Probably its major attribute is excellent management by the Stapf-Neubert family who oversee every detail of the operation and take personal responsibility to ensure that everyone is properly pampered. I spoke to Mr. Neubert who told me that his great grandfather came from Copenhagen in 1885 and bought the castle which became so popular with his visiting friends that it soon became a prosperous hotel. The lounges and dining rooms are not fancy, but have a lived-in, comfortable ambiance. Many fresh foods are included in the menu and both red and white wine, produced from the inn's own vineyards, are served with meals. The central staircase dramatically leads upstairs where there are 35 bedrooms - many with lovely mountain views. The setting of this old castle is peaceful and quiet, and if you enjoy being in the countryside, you will delight in the marvelous network of walking paths leading in every direction.

HOTEL CASTEL LABERS
Owner: Stapf-Neubert Family
Via Labers, 25
39012 Merano, Italy
tel: (0473) 34484 fax: (0473) 34146
32 rooms: Lire 170,000-190,000
Open end of March to November
Credit cards: AX DC MC
Overlooks valley and mountains
Swimming pool, good for families
In the countryside 7 km S of Merano
28 km NW of Bolzano

If you love picturesque chalet-style hotels in quiet, isolated surroundings, then the Hotel Vigiljoch will definitely be your cup of tea. There is absolutely no highway noise: there are no cars. The only way to reach the hotel is by cable car which you take from the town of Lana which is near Merano in the mountains of northeastern Italy. The cable car rises quickly from the floor of the valley and has a breathtaking view of the vineyards and apple orchards. When the cable car reaches the top and slowly joggles into the terminal you will see the Hotel Vigiljoch just to the left of the station. In summer, flowers will be bursting from every window and umbrellas will be gaily decorating the front terrace. Inside you will find quite simple bedrooms, but many of which have balconies with a sweeping view of valley and mountain. The bedrooms are small but pleasantly furnished with furniture painted in an Alpine motif. A sprinkling of antiques highlights the lounges. My very favorite room is an intimate, wood-paneled dining room whose wonderful country prints of blue and red are complimented by attractive light-pine furniture.

HOTEL VIGILJOCH
Owner: Karl Gapp
39011 Vigiljoch
Lana bei Merano, Italy
tel: (0473) 51236 fax: (0473) 51410
35 rooms: Lire 168,000 for 2 persons
Rates include breakfast & dinner
Open March 15 to November 15
Credit cards: none accepted
Mountaintop setting, pool
Accessible only by cable car
9 km S of Merano on route 238
24 km NW of Bolzano

The Villa di Monte Vibiano is unique: we have nothing else quite like it in our Italian guide.   Not a hotel at all, but rather an exquisite private castle that opens its doors to paying guests.   And indeed you will feel like a pampered guest from the moment you enter into the huge entrance hall and are greeted by the English butler.   There are only six guest rooms so staying here is like being at a weekend "house party", especially since dinner (including wine) is included in the price and guests eat family style in the gorgeous dining room.   Staying at the villa is expensive, but not when compared to the prices of deluxe hotels in Rome or Florence, and here you are getting the chance to truly live the life of nobility in an Italian castle.   The Villa di Monte Vibiano is visible from miles around as it is spectacularly located on the crest of a wooded hilltop, affording sensational panoramic views of the countryside in every direction.   While staying at Monte Vibiano, the castle is your home.   You can wander through the gorgeously decorated rooms, literally a museum of stunning antiques, sit and read a book in one of the cozy nooks, play cards in the game room, swim in the refreshing pool, or walk in complete seclusion through the woods.   There is also a very old garden maze, an outdoor theater, and even a tree house accessible to guests.

VILLA DI MONTE VIBIANO
Owner: Andrea Fasola Bologna
Monte Vibiano, 06050 Mercatello, Italy
tel: (075) 8783371
6 rooms: U.S. $420.00 (for 2 persons)
Rate includes breakfast & dinner & all drinks
Swimming pool, sensational views
Listed on Hallwag map under Monte Vibiano
25 km S of Perugia
1 km south of Mercatello

Finding a hotel with even a minimum of charm and personality is certainly no easy feat in Milan, a city which caters primarily to business travellers rather than tourists. Yet, being a hub of so many direct airline flights, Milan sorely needs overnight accommodations. One suggestion is the Hotel Manzoni with its superb location on Via Santo Spirito between the Via Montenapoleono and the Via della Spiga. The newer construction, squeezed between older buildings, has been a hotel since the 1950's. The courteous and attentive owner, Signor Renato, holds a great admiration for his native city, manifested through the many photo reproductions of Milan from the 1800's hung throughout the hotel. Decorated in a simple and classic style, the entrance with spiral staircase takes one down to the not-particularly-attractive "blue bar" where a late night snack is served. The upper floors are color coded in subdued hues of green, blue, beige or orange with linen fabric lining walls and armoires of rooms furnished with wicker or leather pieces. Reserve well in advance.

HOTEL MANZONI
Owner: Renato Gilli
Via Santo Spirito 20
20121 Milan, Italy
tel: (02) 76005700 fax: (02) 784212
45 rooms: Lire 160,000
Closed August
Credit cards: none accepted
In the heart of Milan

During the 17th and 18th Centuries it was fashionable for wealthy Venetian noble-men to build palatial retreats along the cool banks of the Brenta River, thus the waterway became lined with sensational villas all the way from Venice to Padua. Today villages and commerce have built up in the area, but many of the mansions still survive, filled with statues, frescos, and Murano glasswork, attesting to the opulent life-style of days gone by. Some are now open as museums, but for those who really want to experience living the noble life as in the past, there is the lovely 17th-century Villa Margherita, an elegant small hotel. It is situated across the highway from the canal, just a short stroll from one of the villa museums, and a short drive from the others. Many converted villas in Italy are beautiful but faded, reflecting gentile neglect. Not so with the Villa Margherita where all is beautifully maintained; every detail is perfect. From the lounges with their elegant antiques to the guest rooms with color coordinated fabrics, each detail shows the care and involvement of the owner, Valeria Sabbadin, an expert hotelier. Far from the hubbub of Venice, yet only a 20 minute drive away, the Villa Margherita is an excellent hotel choice for those who prefer to avoid the hustle and bustle of the city. If you go into Venice to see the sights, it is best to take the bus, thus avoiding the congestion of traffic and high expense of parking.

HOTEL VILLA MARGHERITA
Owner: Valeria & Remingio dal Corso
Via Nazionale 416
30030 Mira, Italy
tel: (041) 4265800 fax: (041) 4265838
19 rooms: Lire 200,000-220,000
Open all year
Credit cards: all major
On canal 2 km W of Mira
20 km W of Venice, 15 km E of Padua

Of course, it is fun to be in the heart of Venice, but for half the price of what you would pay for a first class hotel there, you can stay twenty minutes to the north at the Villa Condulmer, a splendid 17th-century villa whose rooms more closely resemble a museum than a hotel. The rooms are grand, with fabulous wall frescos painted by Moretti Laresi. The eight rooms in the original villa are the most sumptuous in decor; however, in the heat of summer you might prefer the newer wing whose rooms provide the option of air conditioning. There are several lovely dining rooms for you to enjoy. In addition, when the weather is balmy, you may choose to have your meals served outdoors on the terrace. In the garden is a large pool and nearby a gym set which would appeal to children. For adult "play", there is a golf course adjacent to the hotel where arrangements can be made for you to play if you have a letter of introduction from your club in the United States. Should you like horseback riding this too can be arranged.

VILLA CONDULMER
Manager: Mr. Chinellato
31021 Mogliano Veneto, Italy
tel: (041) 457100 fax: (041) 457134
45 rooms: Lire 176,000-186,000
Closed Jan 7 to February 15
Credit cards: all major
Pool, tennis, play yard, golf
Good stopover for children
4 km NE of Mogliano toward Zerman
18 km N of Venice

The Castello di Gargonza is a romantic walled, storybook village, surrounded by forests and perched at the crest of a hill. The 900-year-old complex of stone buildings now receives guests. There are 7 guest rooms for overnight guests plus 19 picturesque farmhouses available for rent by the week. Most have one or two bedrooms plus a kitchenette and many also have a fireplace - perfect for chilly evenings. Each small cottage is named and when you make a reservation, the hotel will send you a map of the town and a description and a sketch of each of the houses so that you can choose what most appeals to your needs. If you prefer not to cook, there is a restaurant called "La Torre di Gargonza". The village oozes with charm: staying here is like stepping back to medieval times. The interior decor leaves something to be desired, with an extensive use of plastic furniture interspersed with more traditional pieces. However, the overall ambiance is terrific and the hotel is a fabulous bargain, especially for two couples travelling together or families with children who want a home base for exploring Tuscany. Note: The closest town on the Hallwag map is Monte Savino; the hotel is actually located about 8 kilometers west, on road 73 to Siena.

CASTELLO DI GARGONZA
Owner: Count Roberto Guicciardini
Manager: Giuliano Fucini
Azienda Castello di Gargonza
52048 Monte San Savino, Arezzo, Italy
tel: (0575) 847021   fax: (0575) 847054
7 rooms: Lire 160,000-216,000 (3 day minimum)
19 apartments: Lire 595,000-1,382,000 per week
Closed month of January
Restaurant closed Tuesdays
Credit cards: AX
35 km E of Siena, 8 km W of Monte Savino, rte 73

La Chiusa, nestled in the hills of Tuscany southeast of Siena, is an old stone farmhouse whose restaurant is so famous that guests come from miles away to enjoy the meals where everything is known to be fresh, homemade, and delicious. Dania and Umberto Lucherini are the gracious owners and Dania is the talented chef. Almost all the vegetables, olive oil, meats, wines, and cheeses either come from the inn's own farm or from those nearby. The original woodburning oven still stands in the courtyard in front of the inn, emitting delicious aromas of freshly baking bread. The dining room is large and airy, with an uncluttered simple elegance enhanced by windows overlooking rolling hills. When the weather is balmy, meals are also served on the back terrace which is ideally positioned with a sweeping view. The emphasis here is definitely on the exquisite meals, but happily there are also seven bedrooms for guests who want to spend the night. Like the dining room, the guest rooms are perfectly in keeping with the ambiance of the old farmhouse, lovely in their rustic simplicity yet with every modern convenience. If you appreciate and are willing to pay for gourmet meals, La Chiusa makes a perfect base for exploring Tuscany.

LA CHIUSA
Owner: Lucherini Family
Manager: Sodi Franco
Via della Madonnina 88
53040 Montefollonico (Siena), Italy
tel: (0577) 669668 fax: (0577) 669593
7 rooms: Lire 250,000, 2 apartments: Lire 340,000
Open Mar 15 - Nov 5 & Dec 7 - Jan 7
Credit cards: all major
Gourmet restaurant with rooms
60 km S of Siena
10 km NW of Montepulciano

Lucia Ana Luhan, whose parents came from Italy, grew up in a family rich in Italian tradition.　She now lives in California where she is married to a busy surgeon, has a family of three, and operates several very successful fresh pasta restaurants plus a catering service.　For most women this would keep them *more* than busy.　But you don't know Lucia.　A few years ago, while on holiday in Italy, she fell in love with a 500-year-old stone farmhouse, bought it on a whim, and converted it into the Bed & Breakfast of Tuscany.　Now Lucia commutes back and forth between California and Italy.　When Lucia is not at her Italian farmhouse, it is well-managed by Renata Cerchiari.　However, if Lucia is in residence, that fact alone is reason enough to visit because pretty Lucia's radiant personality fills her small bed and breakfast.　This seven bedroom inn is not luxurious, nor is it meant to be.　All of the rooms are decorated in a homey, comfortable way - nothing contrived, just naturally pleasing and in keeping with the rustic nature of the simple stone house. When the weather is mild, guests enjoy a bountiful breakfast outside on the terrace where they congregate again in the late afternoon to sip cool drinks while sharing the day's adventures.　In the evening, if requested, a simple supper of homemade soup, cheeses and cold cuts is available.　Or, for guests who want a fancier dinner, the world-famous spa town of Montecatini is just a 6-minute drive down the hill. Monsummano Terme is the closest town to Montevettolini on the Hallwag map.

BED & BREAKFAST OF TUSCANY
Owner: Lucia Ana Luhan
144 Via dei Bronzodi
51010 Montevettolini, Italy
7 rooms: $150 U.S. dollars
tel & fax: (0572) 628817
Open all year
Credit cards: none accepted
55 km E of Florence, 3 km NW of Monsummano

The town of Orvieto, just off the main expressway between Rome and Florence, is one of the most picturesque of all the Umbrian hilltowns. The small city crowns the top of a hill - an intriguing sight which can be viewed from miles away. Less than a 10-minute drive south of Orvieto is a 12th-century Gothic abbey which has been converted into a hotel. Here you can stay surrounded by the romantic ruins of yesteryear. We have overnighted at La Badia, enjoying the pool and the "old-world" atmosphere. Some readers have written they too liked their stay at La Badia, but we continue to receive some letters complaining of the aloof attitude of the personnel. Although La Badia does not seem to exude the caring management that makes staying at a hotel special, the location near the stunning town of Orvieto is excellent. The hotel itself is nice: the dining room is especially attractive with an enormous, high vaulted stone ceiling, wrought iron fixtures, heavy wooden beams, eye-catching copper accents and, at one end, a cavernous fireplace complete with a spit for roasting. The bedrooms are not large, but are comfortable and many have a stunning view of the town of Orvieto. In the meadows behind the monastery there is a pool which makes a welcome respite from a day on the road.

LA BADIA
Owner: Family of Count Giuseppe Fiume
05019 Orvieto Scalo, Italy
tel: (0763) 90359 fax: (0763) 92796
24 rooms: Lire 263,000
Open March through December
Credit cards: all major
Restaurant closed Wednesdays
Pool, tennis, good for children
4 km S of Orvieto, 115 km N of Rome

The Villa le Barone was once the home of the famous Tuscan family, Della Robbia, whose delightful terra cottas are still seen throughout Italy.   Most of the estate now has been beautifully converted into a deluxe small hotel, but the present owner, Duchessa Franca Viviani Della Robbia, still maintains a charming vine covered cottage for her own use.   Although she is now in her eighties, the Duchessa comes frequently to the villa to ensure that her impeccable standards and exquisite taste prevail.   Staying at the Villa le Barone is very much like being the fortunate guest in a private, elegant home set in the gorgeous Tuscany hills.   There are only 25 guest rooms, all of which vary in size and decor, but each with an individual charm. In addition, there is a lovely pool on a terrace overlooking the vineyards and out to the mellow hills beyond.   Wonderful little terraces are found secluded in the park-like setting where guests can find a quiet nook to read or just to sit and soak in the beauty.   The food is divine and in balmy weather lunch can be taken in the garden and dinner perhaps inside in a charming dining room which formerly housed the stables.   Reservations are accepted for a minimum of three nights, but that should be no problem - three nights will be too short an interlude to spend in this romantic paradise.   (Closest town on Hallwag map, Greve)

VILLA LE BARONE
Owner: Duchessa Franca Viviani Della Robbia
Manager: Caterina Buonamici
Via San Leolino, 19
50020 Panzano in Chianti, Italy
tel: (055) 852215   fax: (055) 852277
25 rooms: Lire 300,000-340,000 *
* Rates include breakfast & dinner
Open Easter through October
Villa in the Tuscany hills
31 km S of Florence, 6 km S of Greve

My first introduction to La Scuderia, beautifully situated in the heart of Tuscany, was one idyllic evening while sitting outside in the garden with friends enjoying a simple, yet delicious dinner.   Perhaps the magic was the balmy air, the delicate wine or just the home cooked meal.   It was not until later that we learned that in addition to the restaurant (which is managed by a young local couple, Rossella and Marco), there are three apartments for rent.   The suite in the back is one of my favorite hideaways in Tuscany.   Here you will find a plain little old-fashioned parlor, a large bathroom (with a tiny little bathtub), a cheerful, well-supplied kitchen with a table tucked in the corner for dining, and a romantic bedroom which is simply, but attractively, furnished in family antiques with the added bonus of a "Romeo and Juliet" balcony overlooking the garden and vineyards.   The apartments are best suited for a stay of a week (breakfst not included in weekly rate), but guests will be taken on a bed and breakfast basis for a three-day minimum.   La Scuderia is not a sophisticated, luxurious hotel, but for those who enjoy simple accommodation and appreciate genuine, home-like hospitality, this is a real winner.   Note: The closest town on Hallwag map is Sambuca.

LA SCUDERIA
Owners: Stella & Carlo Casolaro
Badia a Passignano
50020 Sambuca Val di Pesa, Italy
tel: (055) 8071524
3 apartments: Lire 600,000 per week
Double Lire 80,000 by the night *
 * 3 day day minimum
Open all year
Restaurant closed Wednesdays
Credit cards: None accepted
32 km S of Florence, 5 km NE of Sambuca

How smug I felt at "discovering" the Castel Pergine, for here is a picturebook castle perfect for the budget-minded tourist. No need to forfeit romance and glamour for even though the Castel Pergine is inexpensive, it has a fabulous location dominating a hilltop above the town of Pergine. Luckily, this castle has been delightfully transformed into a small hotel with incredible views out over the valleys and wooded hills. From the tower you can even see two small lakes in the distance which invite a picnic. The Castel Pergine is more famous as a restaurant than a hotel, in fact the Michelin guide gives the kitchen a two fork rating. The dining room has an engaging medieval decor, gorgeous views, and good food. In another wing of the castle the guest rooms offer accommodation ranging from rather basic to comfortably charming. About half of the 21 rooms have private baths; these are more expensive but also more appealingly decorated with handsome wooden panelling and rustic, country-style furnishings. All the guest rooms are pleasant, most offering lovely views, but room #27, a corner room, is especially large and pretty. The Castle Pergine is a real bargain for the price-conscious traveller, its secluded hilltop ambiance definitely a winner - especially if you are travelling with children who will love their "own" Disneyland-like castle.

CASTEL PERGINE
Owner: Fontanari Family
38057 Pergine, Italy
tel: (0461) 531158
21 rooms: Lire 130,000
Rate includes 3 meals a day
Open May to October 15
Ancient castle - lovely views
Hilltop castle - good choice for families
71 km S of Bolzano, 2.5 km E of Pergine

I am such a romantic that, as the boat chugged across the lake from Stresa to the medieval fishing village of Isola dei Pescatori and I saw the Hotel Verbano with its reddish-brown walls, dark green shutters, and tables set on the terrace overlooking the lake, my heart was won - completely.   The lobby is a bit shabby with its rather lumpy and worn furniture; however, the room then opens onto a very nice dining room whose arched windows overlook Lake Maggiore.   A second dining area is set up on the terrace with romantic views of the lake.   Upstairs the twelve bedrooms vary considerably.   One I saw was quite drab but another was very charming with hand painted furniture.   The views from some of the bedrooms are very nice. The Hotel Verbano has a marvelous restaurant.   When we first visited, the same cook had been creating meals for 28 years.   Unfortunately, she is now gone, but the owners wrote that they still have an excellent kitchen featuring wonderful home-style Italian cuisine and freshly caught fish from the lake.   This is not a hotel for those who want everything "perfect", but for those who love a romantic setting at a not-too-expensive price, this special small hotel has great appeal.

HOTEL VERBANO
Owner: Zacchera Family
Via Ugo Ara, 2
28049 Isola dei Pescatori, Stresa
Borromee Isole, Lake Maggiore, Italy
tel: (0323) 30408 fax: (0323) 33129
12 rooms: Lire 132,000
Open March to November
Credit cards: all major
Lovely lakefront restaurant
Island in Lake Maggiore
80 km NW of Milan, ferry from Stresa

Taking a small road that winds up the hill from the non-descript hamlet of Pievescola, you soon see on your left a big gate leading into a large courtyard faced by a lovely old villa-castle and a church.   You check into the inn across the street from the gate where, to the left of the restaurant, there is a small door with a sign, "Hotel Relais La Suvera - Reception".   The noble Ricci family live in one part of the villa.   The other section is efficiently managed by Hilda Zeri as an elegant bed and breakfast.   Some parts of the palace date from the 14th Century, others from the 16th Century exhibiting a combination of styles, incorporating Renaissance arcades with older, more fortress-like architecture.   The public rooms and bedrooms are furnished with dramatic family antiques and an astounding museum-quality art collection.   There is not a feeling of this being a slickly run, sophisticated operation: as a result, guests have the sensation of actually living the noble life of a by-gone era.   In addition to the guest rooms in the villa, there are others available in the former olive processing house (where you check in) and in the converted horse stables.   Although very pleasant, these rooms are less stately than those in the main house.   The restaurant, "Oliviera", is located in the former olive pressing building, and serves traditional Tuscan cuisine as well as other specialties.   The wine cellar is extensive, featuring wines produced in vineyards dating from the 12th Century.

LA SUVERA
Owner: Marchese Giuseppe Ricci
Pievescola, Casole d'Elsa
53030 Siena, Italy
34 rooms: Lire 235,000-400,000
tel: (0577) 960008 fax: (0577) 960220
Credit cards: all major
Swimming pool, restaurant
30 km W of Siena, 16 km E of Casole d'Else

It has become increasingly difficult to find a hotel in Rome with thick enough windows to keep out the ever-present buzz of traffic. Less than an hour's drive from the city, the Borgo Paraelios offers *the perfect* solution: a luxurious country villa immersed in the lovely Tuscan-like hills of Sabinia. In this splendid villa, filled to the brim with elegant antiques, rich, warm-colored tapestries and period paintings, it is impossible to find a detail overlooked. It is a masterpiece of harmonizing old and new, as antique terra cotta tile floors, stone fireplaces, beamed ceilings and antique doors from castles and villas were actually brought here and cleverly incorporated into the building. The very inviting bedrooms, each with its own character and color scheme, look out over the lush garden where guests can breakfast among the flower-laden cotta vases. Meandering through the gracious living room, two libraries, billiard and bridge rooms, one has the sense of having been invited to the country home of nobility for a weekend of absolute peace and tranquility. An additional service is daily transportation to and from Rome, including an apartment near the Spanish Steps at guests' disposal for lunching and freshening up during siesta hours in the city. When you return from the bustle of the city, exquisite meals are served in the frescoed formal dining room.

HOTEL BORGO PARAELIOS
Owner: Signori Salabe
Loc. Valle Collicchia
02040 Poggio Mirteto Scalo (RI), Italy
tel: (0765) 26040 fax: (0765) 26068
12 rooms: Lire 350,000
Open all year
Credit cards: all major
45 km NE of Rome, 2 km N of Poggio Mirteto
U.S. Rep: Hidden Treasures of Italy
Rep tel: (708) 853-1312

The Relais El Toula is a tiny, ten-room, super deluxe, exquisite inn located less than an hour's drive north of Venice. Just to be included in the elegant "Relais et Chateaux" hotel association almost automatically means a divine hotel. The Relais El Toula is not only a member of this prestigious family of hotels, but is also rated one of their most deluxe hotels in Italy. The villa has an idyllic, country setting. The original villa is flanked by two arcaded wings which stretch to the sides giving the building an elegant, long, low image. After driving through the vineyards you arrive at an iron gate through which you enter into a courtyard and the hotel. Inside there is an abundance of fresh flowers in the lounges and delightful bedrooms. In addition to the lovely park-like setting and the beautiful rooms, there is another bonus - the food and wines are superb. It is not surprising that the hotel is so exceptional, for it was owned by Alfredo Beltrame, a real pro in the inn-keeping profession. He was the founder of the Toula hotel chain.

RELAIS EL TOULA
Director: Giorgio Zamuner
Via Postumia, 63
31050 Ponzano, Treviso, Italy
tel: (0422) 969191 fax: (0422) 969994
10 rooms: Lire 315,000-410,000
Open all year
Credit cards: AX DC VS
Lovely villa, own vineyards, pool
2 km N of Ponzano Veneto toward Paderno
35 km N of Venice, 5 km NW of Treviso

The Al Vecchio Convento is a real gem, offering quality accommodation for a moderate price. Its several dining rooms are brimming with rustic country charm and serve delicious meals prepared from local produce. There are nine guest rooms, each with a private bathroom and each tastefully decorated with antiques. The town of Portico de Romagna is, like the inn, inviting yet unpretentious - a very old village surrounded by wooded hills and clear mountain streams. A stroll through medieval pathways that twist down between the weathered stone houses leads you to an ancient stone bridge gracefully arching over a rushing stream.   The inn too is very old.   At first I thought its origin must have been an old convent because of its name, but the wonderfully gracious owner, Marisa Raggi, told me that the name came from a restaurant, located in a convent, that she and her husband, Giovanni (who is the chef), used to operate.   Later, when they moved the restaurant to its present location and added a few guests rooms, they kept the original name, Al Vecchio Convento.   The restaurant is still their main focus, featuring fine meals beautifully prepared from local produce.   Due to the winding, two lane mountain highway which leads to the village, it takes about two hours to drive from Florence, but if you enjoy the adventure of exploring Italy's back roads, this small hotel will certainly be one of your favorites as it is mine.

ALBERGO AL VECCHIO CONVENTO
Owner: Marisa Raggi & Giovanni Cameli
Via Roma, 7
47010 Portico di Romagna, Italy
tel: (0543) 967752 fax: (0543) 967877
9 rooms: Lire 90,000
Open all year
Credit cards: AX DC VS
Restaurant closed Wednesdays
75 km NE of Florence, 34 km SW of Forli

The Il Pellicano has been beautifully designed in the traditional villa style and, although not old, looks as though it has snuggled on its prime hillside position overlooking the Mediterranean for many years.   The facade is of stucco, painted a typical Italian russet and set off by a heavily tiled roof.   Vines enwrap the building, further enhancing its inviting look.   One enters into a spacious, attractive lobby where the sun streams through the windows enhancing the white walls, terra cotta floors, and wooden beamed ceilings.   The happy ambiance continues with pretty sofas, antique accents, and enormous displays of fresh flowers enlivening every conceivable nook and cranny.   The overall impression is one of light and color - and great taste.   Beyond the reception area is an outdoor dining terrace, a favorite place to dine when the weather is balmy.   Frequently the chef serves elaborate buffets outside - (the food at Il Pellicano is expensive, but excellent.)   From the terrace, a lawn dotted with trees extends down the hillside to where there is a beautiful pool romantically perched at the cliff's edge.   From the pool a staircase leads to a pier at the water's edge.   Along this path, small individual terraces with lounge chairs and mats for sunning have been built into the rocks.   In front of the hotel is a tennis court, again surrounded by flowers.   The Il Pellicano is expensive but superb - a truly idyllic retreat.

IL PELLICANO
Managers: Ennio & Nadia Emili
58018 Porto Ercole, Italy
tel: (0564) 833801   fax: (0564) 833418
30 rooms: Lire 220,000-600,000
Open April to end September
Credit cards: all major
Tennis, swimming pool, ocean swimming
South end of island, Hwy 1 exit Orbetello
160 km N of Rome, 4.5 km S of Porto Ercole

The Splendido is truly a luxury hotel. Located up a winding, wooded road high above the town of Portofino, it sits majestically above the beautiful blue Mediterranean and overlooks the boats which are moored in Portofino's lovely harbor. The hotel is much like a very stately, wealthy country home. On a terrace below the hotel is an enormous swimming pool. There is also a tennis court located in the gardens to the left of the hotel. The public rooms are charming with comfortable chairs covered with floral prints and fresh flowers galore. There is a delightful outdoor terrace where meals are served. The bedrooms too are lovely and many have balconies which overlook the sea. There are also romantic little pathways originating from the hotel. You can stroll the wooded grounds and stop along the way at strategically placed benches to enjoy incomparable views. The Splendido is deluxe and veru expensive, but it is a beautiful hotel. If you love luxury and desire a resort setting in one of the most naturally scenic parts of Italy, you will certainly enjoy the marvelous Splendido.

HOTEL SPLENDIDO
Manager: Antonio Marson
16034 Portofino, Italy
tel: (0185) 269551 fax: (0185) 269614
65 rooms: from Lire 693,000
Rate includes breakfast & dinner
Credit cards: all major
Closed October 28 to March 28
Beautiful swimming pool, tennis
5 km S of Santa Margherita Ligure
35 km E of Genoa

The Albergo Casa Albertina is a prime example of what a difference management can make.   There is a wide choice of hotels in the picturesque little fishing village of Positano - many, like the Casa Albertina, with spectacular views, pleasant decor, and good meals.   However, they don't have Michele Cinque who is an outstanding hotelier: gracious and   warmhearted - willing to do whatever is required to make each guest feel very special.   It is not surprising that Michele is such a pro - he has been in the hotel business for many years, having been the manager of one of Positano's most deluxe hotels (Le Sirenuse) before deciding to spend full time helping his wife and mother-in-law manage the Casa Albertina.   The hotel is really a family operation: Michele is usually at the front desk ready to care for the guests, his mother-in-law is in charge of the kitchen while his wife helps out wherever needed.   Two sons are also working at the hotel and one of them has already taken over its official management - and quite ably, I might add.   The hotel (which is built into a 12th-century house) clings to the hillside above Positano, a position which affords superlative views, but also means a strenuous walk into town.

ALBERGO CASA ALBERTINA
Manager: Lorenzo Cinque
Via Tavolozza, 4
84017 Positano, Italy
tel: (089) 875143   fax: (089) 811540
20 rooms: Lire 240,000-280,000 high season
Rates include breakfast & dinner
Open all year
Credit cards: all major
Beautiful views from all of the rooms
55 km S of Naples, 17 km S of Sorrento

For those who want to be smack in the middle of the colorful fishing village of Positano, the Palazzo Murat might be just your cup of tea.   It is superbly located - surrounded by shops and only steps down to the beach.   The hotel consists of two parts: the original building (a 200-year-old palace) plus a new wing which stretches out as an extension to the side.   The new section is a standard hotel - pleasant but not unusual.   However, the palace is quite special, with a faded-pink patina whose charm is accented by wonderful arched alcoves, intricately designed windows and magenta bougainvillea clinging to the walls and cascading from the wrought iron balconies.   The entrance to the hotel is through a sun-drenched patio, a favorite gathering spot for guests.   Within, the "old-world" feeling is maintained with tiled floors, white walls and formal settings of antique sofas and chairs.   Upstairs, in the palace section, are five bedrooms, some with wonderful French doors opening onto small balconies which capture a view of the bay.   The rooms in the original building have no air conditioning, but the walls are so thick they supposedly form their own insulation against the heat.   The only meal served is breakfast: this is actually a bonus since there are so many quaint restaurants in Positano enticingly nearby.   At the time we visited the hotel, plans were being made to upgrade it into a higher category - if this has happened the price might unfortunately have increased significantly from what is shown below.

HOTEL PALAZZO MURAT
Owners: Attanasio Family
Via dei Mulini, 23
84017 Positano, Italy
tel: (089) 875177 fax: (089) 811419
28 rooms: Lire 180,000-210,000
Open Easter to October 15
Near the beach - heart of Positano
55 km S of Naples, 17 km S of Sorrento

The Il San Pietro di Positano is touted as one of the most delightful deluxe hotels in the world. It is. There is no question about it. From the moment you approach the hotel "class" is evident: no large signs; no gaudy advertising; just an ancient chapel along the road indicates to the knowledgeable that an oasis is below the hill. After parking in the designated area near the road, you take an elevator which whisks you down to the lounge and lobby. You walk out of the elevator to a dream world - an open spacious world of sparkling white walls, tiled floors, colorful lounge chairs, Oriental rugs, antique chests, flowers absolutely everywhere, and arches of glass through which vistas of greenery and sea appear. To the right is a bar and to the left is a marvelous dining room - again with windows of glass opening to the view, but with the outdoors appearing to come in, with the walls and ceilings covered with plants and vines. The bedrooms too seem to be almost a Hollywood creation - more walls of glass, bathrooms with views to the sea, and balconies on which to sit and dream. If you can tear yourself away from your oasis of a bedroom, an elevator will whisk you down the remainder of the cliff to the small terrace at the water's edge. If all this sounds gaudy, it isn't. It is perfect.

IL SAN PIETRO DI POSITANO
Owners: Salvatore & Virginia Attanasio
84017 Positano, Italy
tel: (089) 875455 fax: (089) 811449
55 rooms: Lire 522,000-605,000
Rates include breakfast & dinner
Closed December to March 14
Credit cards: all major
Swimming pool
Just south of Positano on Amalfi Drive
55 km S of Naples, 17 km S of Sorrento
U.S. Rep: E&M: 800-223-9832

Le Sirenuse is a superb luxury hotel tucked smack in the middle of the picturesque ancient fishing village of Positano.   It is no wonder that so many writers and artists have been attracted to this colorful town of brightly hued houses clinging to the precipitous hillside as it drops down to its own small bay.   And it is also no wonder that so many of these men of fame have found their way to the oasis of Le Sirenuse. From the moment you enter the hotel lobby the mood is set with fresh white walls, tiled floors, oil paintings on the walls, and accents of antiques.   The hotel cascades down the hill and so almost all the rooms capture a wonderful view out over the quaint rooftops and the tiled domed cathedral to the shimmering blue waters of the bay.   It is only a short walk through the perpendicular streets until you are on the beach.   The dining room has walls of glass which allow the maximum enjoyment of the vista below, but most diners prefer the splendor of eating outdoors where the deck is set with tables for dining.   On another level of the hotel there is a small pool for sunning and dipping.

LE SIRENUSE HOTEL
Manager: Luigi Bozza
Via C. Colombo, 30
84017 Positano, Italy
tel: (089) 875066 fax: (089) 811798
60 rooms: Lire 420,000-480,000
Open all year
Credit cards: all major
Swimming pool, delightful views
Old fishing village on Amalfi Drive
55 km S of Naples, 17 km S of Sorrento
U.S. Rep: LHW
Rep tel: 800-223-6800

The Villa Franca, with a commanding position overlooking the sea, is one of Positano's newly renovated classic hotels with an excellent quality/price rapport. There is an immediate warmth and charm as soon as you walk in to the redesigned and redecorated villa. The Russo family wanted to create an attractive full-service hotel without losing the friendliness and service of a small inn. It is just that. The fresh Mediterranean decor is most appealing with royal blue slip-covered armchairs, a profusion of plants, laquered terracotta vases, white tiled floors and walls and arched windows everywhere, so that you don't miss a second of the mesmerizing views of the sea. The elegant glassed-in restaurant with floral tapestry chairs and blue cloths serves fresh local seafood. The bedrooms follow the theme with colorful ceramic tiled floors, cream bedspreads with green and yellow striped trim and to-die-for views. The cherry on top of the cake is the rooftop swimming pool surrounded by yellow chaise lounges and palms with a 360 degree panoramic view over "the world's most beautiful coastline".

HOTEL VILLA FRANCA
Owners: Russo Family
Viale Pasitea, 318
Positano 84017 (SA), Italy
tel: (089) 875655 fax: (089) 875735
29 rooms: Lire 180,000 to 200,000
Restaurant: Breakfast and Dinner served
Open: Easter - October
Credit Cards: all major
Swimming pool, views
55 km S of Naples
18 km S of Sorrento

It was "love at first sight" as I drove up the long graveled road through forest and vineyard and suddenly caught my first glimpse of the Borgo Pretale, a tiny cluster of weathered stone buildings nestled next to their 12th-century watch tower. My first impression was more than justified. This small inn is truly paradise. There is absolute serenity and beauty here with nothing to mar its perfection. Civilization seems miles away as the eye stretches over a glorious vista of rolling hills forested with oaks, juniper and laurel, interspersed with square patches of vineyards. But although this small village is seemingly remote, it is only a short drive south of Siena, thus a perfect hideaway from which to enjoy the magic of Tuscany. And although the buildings seem rustic, this tiny hotel, tucked into a 12th-century hamlet, offers some of the finest accommodations in all of Italy. Each room is a showplace of fine country antiques and splendid designer fabrics, blended together with the artful eye of a skilled decorator. Every piece is selected to create a sophisticated yet rustic elegance. The dining lounge beckons guests to linger after dinner by the roaring fire. A path leads to a groomed tennis court and further on to a swimming pool on a hillside terrace. (Note, Pretale is not on any map we could find, closest town on Hallwag map is Rosia, about 5 km SE of Pretale)

BORGO PRETALE
Manager: Sergio Corrado
53018 localita Pretale-Souicille, Italy
tel: (0577) 345401 fax: (0577) 345625
26 rooms: Lire 350,000-450,000 high season
Open mid-March to mid-November
Credit cards: all major
Swimming pool, tennis
18 km SW of Siena on Rte 73, N on 541
U.S. Rep: Hidden Treasures of Italy
Rep tel: (708) 853-1312

The Relais Fattoria Vignale is a very polished, sophisticated small hotel located in the heart of the Chianti wine region in the small town of Radda.   The hotel was the manor house of one of the large wine estates where the family's wines are still produced and are readily available in a winery shop across the street.   Although located right on the main street near the center of town, there is a country atmosphere because the back of the hotel opens up to lovely views of rolling hills laced with vineyards and dotted with olive trees.   Capturing this idyllic vista is a large swimming pool with comfortable lounge chairs along the side.   Inside, the rooms are all beautifully decorated with a combination of authentic antiques and excellent reproductions.   Care has been taken in the restoration to preserve many of the nice architectural features of the manor such as heavy beams, arched hallways, decorative fireplaces, and painted ceilings.   One of the most appealing of the rooms is an antique library where guests are welcome to browse.

RELAIS FATTORIA VIGNALE
Manager: Silvia Kummer
Via Pianigiani, 15
53017 Radda in Chianti, Italy
tel: (0577) 738300 fax: (0577) 738592
22 rooms: Lire 220,000-300,000
Open April through October
Credit cards: AX VS
Swimming pool
Originally an 18th-century farm
In the heart of Chianti wine region
52 km S of Florence, 31 km N of Siena

The Rasun di Sopra, built in 1578 by Count Heufler, is actually a castle, but not one of the large foreboding castles sometimes found high on mountain peaks. This is a friendly, almost chalet-like castle, located in a sunny mountain valley in north-eastern Italy. Although within a short drive of some of the most dramatic vistas in the Dolomites, the Ansitz Heufler's setting is pretty, but does not include dramatic jagged mountain peaks. However, in winter skiing is nearby and in summer walking trails beckon in every direction. The Ansitz Heufler does not seem geared to English speaking guests although we did find one of the staff with whom we could communicate. But even though language might be a problem, the reception is very friendly and everyone seems eager to please. The inn is popular as a restaurant and there is an especially cozy dining room with very old paneled walls and ceiling, planked wooden floors, leaded glass windows, tables set with pretty linens, and appealing chalet-style chairs with carved heart backs. In the summer, guests sit out on the terrace where refreshing drinks and snacks are served. The staircase leads up to a wide hallway off which are the bedrooms. The bedrooms are all different from one another, but are all attractively furnished in a simple, uncluttered style with a liberal use of dark antiques attractively setting off whitewashed walls and freshly scrubbed wooden floors.

ANSITZ HEUFLER HOTEL
Owner: Mediolalium Vita
Manager: Valentin Paul Huber
Valle di Anterselva
39030 Rasun di Sopra, Italy
tel: (0474) 46288 fax: (0474) 48199
9 rooms: Lire 120,000-160,000
Closed May & November
Credit cards: DC VS
90 km NE of Bolzano, 12 km E of Brunico

It is no wonder that the Hotel Caruso Belvedere has such an especially spectacular site in Ravello - it was built as a palace in the 11th Century by a noble family who probably had their pick of real estate.   The views of the rugged Amalfi coast from the dining terrace perched high in the clouds is gorgeous.   Many of the bedrooms too have vistas.   Although the decor is rather drab, the views just can't be surpassed.   If you choose the Caruso Belvedere, splurge and ask for one of their most deluxe rooms.   These are simply decorated without much style *BUT* they have enormous balconies which stretch the width of the room to capture again the incredibly romantic coast below.   You will wake in the morning to the sound of birds and the scent of flowers intermixed with the fragrance of the vineyards which drifts up from the terraces beneath your balcony.   The Hotel Caruso has more to offer than just its marvelous views.   The dining room offers excellent food including a divine specialty of the house - a delicious chocolate soufflé which will linger in your memory perhaps as long as the view.   The meals are accompanied by wines from the Caruso family vineyards.

HOTEL CARUSO BELVEDERE
Owner: Caruso Family
Via Toro, 52
84010 Ravello, Italy
tel: (089) 857111 fax: (089) 857372
24 rooms: Lire 210,000-248,000 high season
Closed February
Credit cards: AX DC VS
Hilltown above Amalfi coast
66 km S of Naples, 6 km N of Amalfi

The Marmorata Hotel was cleverly converted from the shell of an old paper mill. Only a few of the old paper mills are still in operation, but at one time the Amalfi area was famous for its production of fine paper. The official address of the Marmorata Hotel is Ravello; however, it is not located in the cliff town of Ravello, but rather on the coastal highway. As you are driving north from Salerno to Ravello you will see the sign to the hotel which is snuggled in the rocky cliffs between the road and the sea. As you enter the hotel you notice the nautical theme carried throughout the decor from the chairs in the dining room to the mirrors on the walls. The interior is charming with comfortable leather lounge chairs and small Oriental rugs. There is a lovely terrace plus, on a lower level, snuggled into the rocks, a small swimming pool. The bedrooms are small, but nicely decorated, again with the seafaring motif: the beds seem to be built into captains' sea chests and nautical prints are on the walls. The bathrooms are also small, but modern and attractive. All of the bedrooms have radios, color televisions, telephones, air conditioning and small refrigerators. Many of the rooms have an excellent view of the water and rugged coast.

MARMORATA HOTEL
Owner: Camera d'Afflitto Family
Strada Statale, 163
84010 Ravello, Italy
tel: (089) 877777 fax: (089) 851189
40 rooms: Lire 225,000-255,000
Open April through November
Credit cards: all major
Pool, small pier, waterfront
On the coast below Ravello
62 km S of Naples, 23 km N of Salerno

There is something magical about the Hotel Palumbo, a 12th-century palace now one of the most special hotels in Italy, owned since 1875 by the charming Vuilleumier family. The location is perfect - up in the clouds overlooking the terraced vineyards and beyond to the brilliant blue sea which dances in and out of the jagged rocky coast. The Palumbo is a divine small hotel. The romance begins when you enter the beautiful lobby with its ancient atrium of arched colonnades, green plants flowing from every nook, masses of fresh flowers and beautiful antiques. Each small corner is an oasis of tranquility from the intimate bar to the cozy antique filled tiny lounges. There is a beautiful dining room with a crystal chandelier, bentwood chairs and a fireplace, but usually meals are served on the breathtaking terrace which perches like a bird's nest in the sky. Wherever you dine, the food is superb and the elegantly gracious owner, Pasquale Vuilleumier, frequently pauses at each table - an attentive host seeing to the contentment of each guest. There is a charming garden in the rear with a vine covered terrace overlooking the Amalfi coast. Another tiny patio which captures both the sun and the view is tucked onto the roof of the villa. There are only 20 bedrooms, each individually decorated and appealing with its own personality. A few guest rooms are located in an annex.

HOTEL PALUMBO
Owner: Pasquale Vuilleumier
84010 Ravello, Italy
tel: (089) 857244 fax: (089) 857347
20 rooms: Lire 423,000-506,000
Rates include breakfast & dinner
Open all year
Credit cards: DC VS
Delightful villa - superb views
66 km S of Naples, 6 km N of Amalfi

The Villa Cimbrone is not only a hotel: its gardens are one of Ravello's most famous attractions. The tourist office proclaims, "The Villa Cimbrone, essence of all the enchantment of Ravello, hangs like a swallow's nest on the cliffs." The villa is reached by a delightful ten-minute walk from the main square of Ravello (the signs are well marked to this favorite sightseeing prize). Once through the gates, the villa and its magnificent gardens open up like magic. The gardens are truly superb - if you have ever received a postcard from Ravello, chances are it showed the view from the terrace of the Cimbrone. Most dramatic of all is the belvedere with its stately Roman statues accenting the dazzling view. Luckily, this outstanding villa is also a small hotel. The rooms are of museum quality with furniture "fit for a king". We toured through the marvelous old building which is not open to the public - only to the guests. This fabulous villa was once the prized possession of an English Lord. Later it was sold to the present owner, Marco Vuilleumier, who told us the following romantic tale: toward the end of World War II, the English nobleman (who owned Villa Cimbrone) landed with the Allied troops in Salerno. Somehow he was able to find a jeep, and - you guessed it - wound up the twisting road to see once again his beloved villa.

VILLA CIMBRONE
Owner: Marco Vuilleumier
84010 Ravello, Italy
tel: (089) 857459 fax: (089) 857777
20 rooms: Lire 209,000-264,000
Open April through October
Credit cards: none accepted
Park-like grounds open to the public
10 minute walk to parking in town center
66 km S of Naples, 6 km N of Amalfi

The Villa Maria is perhaps best known for its absolutely delightful terrace restaurant which has a bird's eye view of the magnificent coast. Whereas most of the hotels in Ravello capture the southern view, the Villa Maria features the equally lovely vista to the north. The Villa Maria is easy to find because it is on the same path which winds its way from the main square to the Villa Cimbrone. After parking your car in the main square of Ravello (or at the Hotel Giordano which is under the same ownership) look for the signs toward the Villa Maria. After about a 2-minute walk, you will find the Villa Maria perched on the cliffs to your right. The building is a romantic old villa with a garden stretching to the side where tables and chairs are set - a favorite place to dine while enjoying the superb view. Inside, there is a cozy dining room which overlooks the garden. The bedrooms are furnished with antique pieces including brass beds. The bathrooms have been freshly remodeled and some even have jacuzzi tubs. The hotel is owned by Vincenzo Palumbo whose staff speaks excellent English should you call for a reservation. Vincenzo Palumbo also owns the nearby Hotel Giordano which has a heated pool that can be used free by guests at the Villa Maria. Many readers have written to us saying how gracious and warm a welcome they receive at the Villa Maria. How lucky to be able to have the best of all worlds should you be on a budget - a wonderful view and location plus a charming villa.

VILLA MARIA
Owner: Vincenzo Palumbo
Via s. Chiara, 2
84010 Ravello, Italy
tel: (089) 857255 fax: (089) 857071
12 rooms: Lire 120,000-140,000
Open all year
Credit cards: all major
66 km S of Naples, 6 km N of Amalfi

Only about a half hour's drive from Florence, easily accessible from the A1 to Rome, is the Villa Rigacci, once a private residence, now an inviting small inn. This 16th-century villa is a "picture-perfect" example of a Tuscan villa with its faded pink stucco facade, thick walls, heavy weathered red tile roof, green shuttered windows and park like gardens. The owner, Odette Mege Pierazzi, is personally involved with all aspects of running the inn: she is like a hostess overseeing the needs of her "house guests". In summer, after a day of sightseeing, guests relax in the back garden where a large pool, surrounded by lounge chairs and umbrellas, stretches out on a terraced lawn. Inside, handsome antiques adorn the sitting rooms and library. The dining room is especially appealing and, according to the guests staying at the inn, the chef is excellent. All of the bedrooms have direct dial telephone, color television, small bar and bathroom. Each is individually decorated with very attractive country-style antiques and lovely fabrics creating rooms that blend beautifully with the old world ambiance of the villa. Although I personally prefer the area of Tuscany that stretches directly south of Florence where the villages seem more secluded, the conveniently located Villa Rigacci offers easy access to the expressway and accommodation with charm, hospitality, and warmth. Note: Vaggio is a small town southwest of Reggello.

HOTEL VILLA RIGACCI
Owner: Odette Mege Pierazzi
50066 Vaggio-Reggello (Tuscany), Italy
tel: (055) 8656718 fax: (055) 8656537
20 rooms: Lire 220,000-260,000
Open all year
Restaurant open January 1 to November 15
Credit cards: all major
Swimming pool
30 km SE of Florence, 5 km S of Regello

For those of you who love the enchantment of exploring Italy's romantic lakes by boat and catching the first glimpse of your hotel as your ferry glides into port, the Hotel Sole is definitely for you.   The Hotel Sole is located next to the pier where the ferries dock, in the ancient port of Riva del Garda, on the northern end of Lake Garda.   The city of Riva has mushroomed to accommodate the influx of tourists, but the old section which surrounds the harbor has retained a great deal of medieval charm with colorful old buildings, towers, and cobbled streets.   When we first visited the Hotel Sole it was slightly run-down, but according to the last letter we received from the manager, it has now been completely renovated in a traditional style.   Although this is not a quaint little hotel, it has a pleasant ambiance and is a perfect location for those who want to stay in the medieval town of Riva and explore Lake Garda by boat.   At the rear of the hotel, an outdoor terrace looks out over the lake and all its activity.   Umbrella-canopied tables invite you to sit and dine or just enjoy a hot cup of coffee while watching the show as boats of all shapes, sizes, and colors move in and out of this tiny harbor.

HOTEL SOLE
Manager: Silvano Lattisi
Piazza 3 Novembre, 35
38066 Riva del Garda, Italy
tel: (0464) 552686 fax: (0464) 552811
52 rooms: Lire 160,000-190,000
Suite: Lire 250,000-320,000
Open April 11 to October
Credit cards: all major
Next to the ferry landing
180 km E of Milan, 103 km S of Bolzano

Hotel rates in the center of Rome are usually very expensive, but the Hotel Carriage, tucked into a tiny side street, is both moderately priced and conveniently situated just a short stroll from the bottom of the Spanish steps. From the outside it is a nondescript, sienna-colored building with green shuttered windows opening directly onto the street. The small entry lobby is flanked by a small breakfast room and a formal parlor with ornate furnishings including brocade chairs, an enormous gilt mirror, a fancy chandelier, and elaborately carved tables. The pretty soft blue walls of this room set the color theme for the hotel; the bedrooms I saw that had been redecorated were also done in varying shades of blue. Some of the guest rooms are very small so it is best to pay a bit more and request one of the best twin-bedded rooms. However, no matter what the size, all the rooms have air conditioning, telephone, radio, small refrigerator, and an old world flavor. One of the nicest features of the hotel is a rooftop terrace where on summer evenings guests may sit at tables and enjoy the view over a jumble of tiled roofs to the twin spires of the 16th-century church, Trinita dei Monti. The Hotel Carriage is not luxurious, but offers a less expensive alternative for lodging in Rome.

HOTEL CARRIAGE
Manager: Giampiero Cau
Via delle Carrozze, 36
00187 Rome, Italy
tel: (06) 6990124 fax: (06) 6788279
30 rooms: Lire 215,000
Open all year
Credit cards:
Located near bottom of Spanish steps

For location, the Gregoriana is superb: it is situated on Gregoriana Street which runs into the Piazza Trinita dei Monti at the top of the Spanish Steps. In spite of the perfect location, when I first saw the Gregoriana I just did not see how I could include it in our "inn" book because it has no antique ambiance: in fact, the decor motif might be classified as Chinese with a touch of art deco. However, after staying at this hotel, I just did not see how I could not include it - it is such a unique little inn and has such a sparkle of personality that it brightens the otherwise somewhat impersonal city of Rome. You will not be just one of thousands of tourists in Rome - upon arrival, the concierge will probably already know you by name and will continue to greet you personally as you come and go. Instead of feeling like a face which goes with a key hanging on the wall, you will feel a warmth and intimacy as if you were a guest in a private home. The rooms are simple but very pleasant and, like the lobby, are decorated with a touch of Oriental ambiance. Those at the rear are especially quiet and some enjoy a balcony with a view over the rooftops of Rome. Only breakfast is served. However, there is a concierge on duty twenty-four hours a day to cater to your special needs.

HOTEL GREGORIANA
Owner: Ernesto Panier-Bagat
Manager: Aldo Basso Bondini
Via Gregoriana, 18
00187 Rome, Italy
tel: (06) 6794269 fax: (06) 6784258
19 rooms: Lire 203,000
Breakfast only meal served
Very personalized service
Located near top of Spanish Steps

The Hotel Hassler is a landmark in Rome. Located in the heart of the elegant shopping area, on the Piazza Trinita dei Monti at the top of the Spanish Steps, this small, elite hotel was once a palatial private home. Its entrance is sedate and elegant. The reception rooms are a little somber, but this mood is quickly relieved by an inner courtyard - a superb oasis with stone walls covered with vines, statues, flowers, cozy little tables, and a bar. You can linger in the garden, take a refreshment in the afternoon or perhaps meet a friend for an aperitif in the evening. The dining room at the Hassler is also spectacular, boasting one of the finest views in Rome: the entire panorama of the city surrounds you as you dine. As the evening deepens and the city lights begin to flicker, the scene will become one of romance. If money is no object, the Hotel Hassler offers some magnificent suites, some with enormous terraces and a view so beautiful that you will be sorely tempted never to set foot from this gorgeous hotel.

HOTEL HASSLER
Manager: Roberto E. Wirth
Trinita Dei Monti, 6
00187 Rome, Italy
tel: (06) 6782651 fax: (06) 6789991
100 rooms: Lire 520,000-700.000
Credit cards: AX VS
Beautiful view restaurant
Located at top of Spanish Steps
U.S. Rep: LHW
Rep tel: 800-223-6800

When we visited the Hotel d'Inghilterra a few years ago, the inside was most appealing although the exterior was quite drab.   On our latest inspection, we were pleased to note that the entrance has been spiffed up and is now much improved. Inside, there is an ambiance of warmth and dignified charm enhanced by strategically placed antiques, lovely paintings decorating the wall, pretty Oriental carpets, antique mirrors and fresh flowers throughout.   Down the hallway is a small bar which seems to be the rendezvous spot for everyone staying at the hotel. This appealing little bar has beautiful dark wood paneling adorned with colorful prints, intimate little tables, fine antique carpets, and comfortable leather sofas. The bedrooms are well decorated in traditional decor.   The location of the d'Inghilterra is excellent.   A short walk in one direction will lead you through lovely shopping avenues to the bottom of the Spanish Steps.   A short walk in the other direction will lead you to the Trevi Fountain with its hubbub of activity. Originally, the Hotel d'Inghilterra was built as a guest house for the famous Torlonia Palace and you will certainly see and appreciate traces of grandeur which are still apparent throughout this once-regal residence.

HOTEL D'INGHILTERRA
Manager: N. Nushin Mozaffari
Via Bocca di Leone, 14
00187 Rome, Italy
tel: (06) 672161 fax: (06) 6840828
102 rooms: Lire 450,000-500,000
Credit cards: all major
Excellent location
Located near foot of Spanish Steps

The Hotel Lord Byron is owned by a fascinating man and superb hotelier, Amedeo Ottaviani, who believes that "Hospitality is like an exquisite flower, it must be surrounded by a thousand delicate attentions" - a concept which transforms each of his hotels into far more than just a place to spend the night. Each is designed to be a "home away from home" - a quiet sanctuary, well-run and full of character. Ottaviani's chain of small, unique hotels includes the Lord Byron - tucked on a tiny lane surrounded by glamorous homes, it is much more like a private townhouse than a commercial establishment. The reception desk is discreetly located in the foyer which opens onto an elegant lounge. An elevator takes guests to the bedrooms, each individually decorated: fabrics, carpets, and the materials used on the custom-built pieces of furniture are carefully chosen to suit the personality and exposure of the room. Most of the furniture is new - modern yet traditional in feel. The colors used in fabrics, wall coverings, and carpets are mostly strong, bold colors - frequently with large, bright floral prints, but consistently of excellent quality. On the lower level is an intimate drawing room-bar where guests can relax before or after dining - adjacent is an elegant restaurant, the Relais Le Jardin, serving without a doubt some of the finest cuisine in Rome.

HOTEL LORD BYRON
Owner: Amedeo Ottaviani
Via G. de Notaris, 5
00197 Rome, Italy
tel: (06) 3220404 fax: (06) 3220405
50 rooms: Lire 380,000-560,000
Open all year
Credit cards: all major
Located on edge of Villa Borghese Park
U.S. Rep: LHW
Rep tel: 800-223-1230

La Residenza was recommended to us by several readers who claimed it to be their favorite place to stay in Rome, and after a personal visit, we are happy to be able to include it in our guide.   This former villa really is quite different from most of the large, commercial places to stay in the center of Rome, appearing to be more like a private residence.   Its facade looks very "Italian" with typical brown shuttered windows, greenery and flowers behind a small paved courtyard where guests may park their cars.   The front hall has been converted into a reception area flanked by several guest lounges.   The decor of these public rooms is not outstanding: some have contemporary, grass-cloth wallpaper, but others are more traditional in feeling and have a smattering of antique furniture.   The breakfast room is spacious, although a bit dark, but the red bentwood chairs add a bit a sparkle. Because the hotel was fully occupied at the time of my visit, I was only able to see a few guest rooms, but those I did see were modern and seemed to be quiet adequate. The location just off the Via Veneto is glamorous, so even though the interior of La Residenza does not abound with charm, it is a good choice for travelers who want a small hotel in a good location without paying a fortune.

LA RESIDENZA
Manager: Mr. d'Arezzo
Via Emilia, 22-24
00187 Rome, Italy
tel: (06) 4880789 fax: (06) 485721
27 rooms: Lire 120,000-215,000
Open all year
Credit cards: all major
No restaurant, breakfast only
Located between Via Veneto and Spanish Steps

The Hotel Sistina is like a breath of Springtime in the captivating yet rather frantic city of Rome. From the moment you walk off the busy street into the charming reception lounge, you will feel as if you are in an elegant country home rather than an impersonal, commercial hotel. This impression of being a guest is further enhanced when, instead of standing in a line in front of a counter to check in, you are cordially invited by the concierge to sit down at a small, antique desk to sign the register (this service I have only encountered before in a few very deluxe hotels). Leading off from the reception area, are two light and airy lounges, appealingly decorated with comfy sofas covered in solid and floral fabrics, puffy pillows, pretty oil paintings in gilt frames, and abundant displays of fresh flowers. Each morning a delicious light buffet breakfast is served in an intimate dining room where round tables are prettily set with cheerful print table clothes and fresh flowers. The bedrooms I saw were not large but spotlessly clean and each with a nice modern bathroom. The miracle of this small hotel is the price. With its superb location at the top of the Spanish steps and the quality of its amenities, one would expect the Sistina to be very expensive. But it is not. After spending several days in Rome inspecting literally dozens of dreary, shabby hotels (most with prices exceeding the Sistina), I was even more impressed at what a gem it is.

HOTEL SISTINA
Owner: Amedeo Ottaviani
Via Sistina, 136
00187 Roma, Italy
tel: (06) 4745000   fax: (06) 4818804
27 rooms: from   Lire 209,000
Open: All year
Credit cards: all major
Located near top of the Spanish Steps
U.S. Rep: Utell International, 800-448-8355

With every new edition of this guide we always add some new hotels; among these a few treasures always stand out, and the Hotel Relais Borgo San Felice is one such gem. Not only is it one of Italy's loveliest country hotels, it is also an outstanding value: a comparable hotel in any of the popular tourist targets would cost much more. Unless you are exclusively a "city person", you will love this hotel. Actually, the name is misleading because it is not a hotel at all in the usual sense of the word, but rather a very old village of beautiful stone buildings which have been cleverly converted into guest rooms, dining rooms, a restaurant and a bar. However, the village is not entirely consecrated to the hotel; local farmers still live in some of the houses and the winery is still housed in its original structure. The San Felice wines, produced on the 2,400 surrounding acres, are some of Italy's finest. All the guest rooms have every amenity and are decorated to offer a traditional ambiance of soft, pleasing colors, floral fabrics and many fine antiques. There is a beautiful swimming pool with a view terrace and also an inviting tennis court tucked into the vineyards. This hotel has no rough edges. It is superbly managed by the gracious Gualtiero Mancini who oversees every detail and welcomes guests with the warmth and friendliness usually only found at small inns. Note: The closest towns found on the Hallwag map are Castelnuovo and Pianella.

HOTEL RELAIS BORGO SAN FELICE
Manager: Gualtiero Mancini
San Felice
53019 Castelnuovo Berardenga, Italy
tel: (0577) 359260 fax: (0577) 359089
51 rooms: Lire 241,000-322,000
Open all year
Credit cards: all major
Swimming pool & tennis
20 km NE of Siena, 9 km NW of Castelnuovo

Finding the appealing Castello Formentini brought us an unexpected bonus: we discovered a niche of Italy which hugs the Yugoslavian border north of Trieste: an absolutely gorgeous region of wooded hills, rolling fields, and vineyards. The Castello Formentini, superbly positioned on a hillock overlooking the countryside, has belonged to the Counts of Formentini since the 16th Century. For many years there has been a restaurant within the castle which still serves excellent meals and a medieval banquet on Saturdays. Recently, just outside the castle walls, one of the historic buildings of the castle complex has been converted into a small, charming luxury inn. The attractive, gracious owner, Isabella Formentini, says that all of the magnificent antique furnishings in the hotel are family heirlooms. Everything is authentic, even the wonderful prints and paintings. In fact, she says the furniture is more valuable than the castle. From the intimate lobby to each of the spacious guest rooms, everything is decorator perfect and exudes a delightful country manor ambiance. Only one of the guest rooms is within the castle, but all the guests can stroll through the gate and into the castle grounds where the swimming pool lies invitingly on the shaded lawn. There is also a tennis court plus a nine hole pitch and putt golf course. Note: The closest town on the Hallwag map is Gorizia.

GOLF HOTEL - CASTELLO FORMENTINI
Owner: Isabella Formentini
San Floriano del Collio
34070 Gorizia, Italy
tel: (0481) 884051 fax: (0481) 884214
13 rooms: Lire 200,000
Open March through December
Credit cards: AX DC VS
Golf, tennis, swimming pool
30 km N of Trieste, 7 km N of Corizia
U.S. Rep: Romantik Hotels 800-826-0015

San Gimignano is one of the most fascinating of the medieval Tuscany hill towns. Most tourists come just for the day to visit this small town.   As you approach, this looks like a city of skyscrapers: come even closer and the "skyscrapers" emerge as 14 soaring towers - dramatic reminders of what San Gimignano must have looked like in all her glory when this wealthy town sported 72 giant towers.   If you are lucky enough to be able to spend the night, San Gimignano has a simple but very charming hotel, La Cisterna.   The hotel is located on the town's main square, and fits right into the ancient character of the surrounding buildings with its somber stone walls softened by ivy, arched shuttered doors, and red tile roof.   Once inside La Cisterna the medieval feeling continues with lots of stone, vaulted ceilings, leather chairs, and dark woods.   The bedrooms are not fancy, but pleasant, and some have balconies with lovely views of the valley.   La Cisterna is probably more famous as a restaurant than as a hotel.   People come from miles around because not only is the food delicious, but the dining rooms are delightful.   Especially charming is the dining room with the brick wall, sloping ceiling supported by giant beams, and picture windows framing the gorgeous Tuscany hills.

LA CISTERNA
Owner: S. Salvestrimi
Piazza della Cisterna, 24
53037 San Gimignano, Italy
tel: (0577) 940328 fax: (0577) 942080
50 rooms: Lire 102,000-112,000
Open March 10 through November 10
Credit cards: all major
Excellent restaurant*
*closed all day Tuesday, Wednesday lunch
Tuesdays & Wednesdays
54 km SW of Florence, 38 km NW of Siena

The Castel San Gregorio is a sensational, small 12th-century stone castle just a short drive from Assisi, reached after following a winding road through a forest which emerges at the top of a hill to a truly romantic, secluded hideaway.   There is a terrace to the side where tables and chairs are strategically placed to capture a splendid view of the valley far below.   The castle, dating from 1140, has been meticulously reconstructed preserving its original appearance without, and maintaining a castle-like ambiance within.   The interior of the hotel is quite dark due both to the character of the building and the wall coverings.   The "old-world" ambiance is further enhanced by the bountiful use of excellent antiques.   The reception desk is in the front lobby: to the left as you enter is an ornate living room; to the right is a dining room where one large table is set each night for the guests to eat together "family style".   A restaurant is located on a lower level, open to the general public, where elegant dining is offered in a beautifully decorated room. The bedrooms I saw, although somewhat dark, were all quite outstandingly decorated with a collection of fine antiques.   Surrounding the hotel are many walking paths leading through the quiet wooded hills.   The Castel San Gregorio is an outstanding value for a hotel with so much character.   Note: The closest town on the Hallwag map is Pianello - its on a small road leading south from town.

CASTEL SAN GREGORIO
Owner: Claudio Bianchi
Via San Gregorio, 16
06081 San Gregorio Pianello, Italy
tel: (075) 8038009 fax: (075) 8038904
12 rooms: Lire 112,000
Closed January
Credit cards: AX DC VS
Wonderful hilltop castle
16 km NW of Assisi, 2 km S of Pianello

The Residence San Sano is a small hotel in San Sano - a hamlet in the center of the Chianti wine-growing region. We were charmed by the hotel which is incorporated into a 16th-century stone building. The gracious young owners, Giancarlo Matarazzo and his German wife, Heidi, were both school teachers in Germany prior to returning to Italy to open a small hotel. They have done a beautiful job in the renovation and in the decor. A cozy dining room serves guests excellent meals - featuring typically Tuscan-style cooking. Each of 11 bedrooms is delightfully furnished in antiques and each has a name incorporating some unique feature of the hotel - the name evolving from the time during reconstruction when Heidi and Giancarlo remembered each room by its special feature. My favorite room was the "Bird Room": here birds had claimed the room for many years and had nested in holes which went completely through the wall. With great imagination, the holes were left open to the outside, but on the inside were covered with glass. Now the birds can still nest and guests have the fun of watching the babies. One room is named for a beautiful, long-hidden Romanesque window which was discovered and incorporated into the decor, another room for its very special view, and another for an antique urn uncovered during renovation. On our latest visit, the inn looked even lovelier than we remembered and a new pool now nestles in the vineyards. Note: The closest town on the Hallwag map is Radda.

HOTEL RESIDENCE SAN SANO
Owners: Heidi & Giancarlo Matarazzo
Loc. San Sano, 53010 Lecchi in Chianti, Italy
tel: (0577) 746130   fax: (0577) 746156
11 rooms: Lire 120,000-132,000
Closed November to mid-March
Credit cards: all major
Swimming pool
60 km S of Florence, 9 km S of Radda

The Locanda San Vigilio is truly special: our favorite among the tiny luxury inns in the beautiful lake district of northern Italy.   And, although it is expensive, it costs less to stay here than at some of the famous well known "queens" along the lake. Not only is it a superb small hotel, but the location is unsurpassed.   The Locanda San Vigilio is a 16th-century building romantically positioned fronting the water on an exquisite, park-like peninsula that juts out into Lake Garda.   There is not much action here.   If you want to see and be seen by the rich and famous, the glamorous Villa d'Este should be your hub, but if you desire tranquility, accented by lovely accommodations, then try the San Vigilio.   Here you will find understated luxury, nothing commercial at all.   Hardly a sign marks the tree-lined entrance just a few kilometers north of the town of Garda.   After parking your car in the designated area, you walk past a gorgeous Italian villa and then down a path to the hotel, a 16th-century sturdy stone building so close to the water that waves gently lap the walls.   The dining room is lovely and if you are lucky, you can eat at one of the cozy tables overlooking the lake.   The food is sensational and the decor is faultless. Upstairs the prize guest rooms overlook the lake.   If you long for tranquility, this is it.   Churchill came here to paint, and after visiting the San Vigilio you may also be inspired to take up the art.

LOCANDA SAN VIGILIO
Owner: Conte Guarienti Agostino
Director: Agostino Guarienti di Brenzone
37016 San Vigilio, Garda, Italy
tel: (045) 7256688   fax: (045) 7256551
7 rooms: Lire 240,000-350,000
Open March to November
Credit cards: all major
Not suitable for children
154 km W of Venice, 3 km N of Garda

The Pitrizza is a tiny jewel of a hotel located on the Emerald Coast of the Island of Sardinia - the playground of the Aga Khan and the jet set of the world.   From the moment you enter through the front gate, marked only with a discreet sign, you are in a world of tranquility and beauty.   There is a central clubhouse which has a beautiful lounge, a delightful dining room with hand-hewn wooden chairs, a card room, and a bar.   A small protected patio extends from the dining room where meals are served when the weather is warm.   French doors from the lounge open onto the terrace which leads down to a most unusual swimming pool, cleverly designed into the natural rock.   Once in this wonderful pool, you have the impression that you are swimming in the sea, not a pool, because the water level matches that of the bay.   The bedrooms are tucked away in small cottages which blend into the landscape.   The rooms are not especially large, but beautiful, with every detail of the finest quality.   If your idea of a vacation is a frenzy of activity and "things to do" then the Pitrizza is definitely not for you.   There are no planned activities, no sports director, no loud music.   Only lovely quiet, gourmet food, a beautiful pool, and a delightful small white sand beach.

PITRIZZA
Manager: Pier Angelo Tondina
07020 Porto Cervo, Sardinia, Italy
tel: (0789) 91500   fax: (0789) 91629
51 rooms: Lire 924,000-1,280,000
Rate includes breakfast & dinner
Open mid-May through September
Credit cards: all major
Pool, beach, tennis available
NE tip of Sardinia, airport Olbia
On the island of Sardinia

Having heard about a lovely little chalet tucked amidst the pines high in the Italian Alps near the French border, I was beginning to wonder what awaited me as the road wound through the ski town of Sauze d'Oulx with its unattractive jumble of modern concrete ski hotels. However, the road soon left the resort town and continued up, twisting higher and higher into the mountains until suddenly Il Capricorno came into view nestled in the forest to the left of the road. Just as you enter there is a tiny bar, and, beyond, a cozy dining room enhanced by dark wooden chalet-style chairs, rustic wooden tables, and a stone fireplace with logs stacked neatly by its side. There is not a hint of elaborate elegance - just a simple cozy country charm: the perfect kind of inn to come "home" to after a day of skiing or walking the beautiful mountain trails. The bedrooms, too, are simple but most pleasant with dark pine handmade furniture, neat little bathrooms, and, for a lucky few, balconies with splendid mountain views. However, the greatest asset of this tiny inn are the owners, Mariarosa and Carlo Sacchi. Carlo personally made most of the furniture and will frequently join the guests for skiing. Mariarosa is the chef, a fabulous gourmet cook. This is a very special little hideaway for very special people.

IL CAPRICORNO
Owners: Mariarosa & Carlo Sacchi
Les Clotes
10050 Sauze d'Oulx, Italy
tel: (0122) 850273
8 rooms: Lire 200,000
Open Jul to Sep 15 & Dec to May
Credit cards: VS
Mountain setting near France
2 km E of Sauze d'Oulx via small lane
60 km W of Turin, 28 km W of Susa

The Maremma, a beautiful area in the coastal foothills of southern Tuscany, quite undiscovered by tourists, offers a wealth of sightseeing possibilities: walled villages, Etruscan ruins, archaeological sites and lovely landscapes. Until recently there were few places to stay with charm. Happily this problem was solved when the Pellegrini family recently converted a 200-year-old stone farmhouse into a small hotel. Here you will find true Tuscany hospitality from the moment you enter. Although the Pellegrinis do not speak English, they have made sure to employ front desk personnel who do. The dining room is the heart of the inn and has tables set in a beamed-ceilinged room that is filled with sunlight from large French doors that open onto a terrace where meals are served on warm days. The guest rooms are small, but comfortable, immaculately clean and each with a private bathroom. The warmth and gracious country-style hospitality of this simple small hotel make a stay here special. Another real bonus is the food. It is wonderful. Everything is homemade, including marvelous pastas prepared by the talented chef, Tullio Sassi, and the hotel even produces its own wines which are served with the meals. A specialty of the inn is trekking (or, as we say, horseback riding). In the coral below the hotel, horses are groomed each day for guests' use; in fact, special room rates are offered which include the use of your own horse.

ANTICO CASALE DI SCANSANO
Owners: Massimo Pellegrini & Family
58054 Castagneta-Scansano (GR), Italy
tel: (0564) 507219   fax: (0564) 507805
16 rooms: Lire 105,000-140,000
Closed January 15 to March 1
Credit cards: AX VS
30 km S of Grosseto, 2 km W of Scansano
U.S. Rep: Hidden Treasures of Italy
Rep tel: 708-853-1312

Although the Berghotel Tirol is a new hotel, it happily copies the typical chalet style of the Dolomites. Inside, too, the tasteful decor follows the delightful Alpine motif with light pine furniture, baskets of flowers, and a few antiques for accent pieces. However, what is so very special about the Berghotel Tirol is its marvelous location on a hillside looking over the lovely village of Sexten and to the fabulous mountains beyond. Many of the rooms have large balconies which capture the view and the warmth of the mountain sun. The Berghotel Tirol is not actually in the town of Sexten (Sesto), but in a suburb called Moos (Moso). This is one of the most scenic areas of the Dolomites and the town of Sexten one of the most attractive of the mountain towns. In addition to the natural beauty, there is a wonderful network of trails leading in every direction to tempt all into the crisp mountain air. When you return at night to the hotel it is rather like a house party. Most of the guests come for at least a week and table hopping is prevalent as the knicker-clad guests share their day's adventures. Acting as hosts to the "house party" are the extremely gracious, cordial owners, the Holzer family, who seem to be dedicated to seeing that everyone has a good time.

BERGHOTEL TIROL
Owner: Kurt Holzer Family
39030 Sexten (Sesto), Italy
tel: (0474) 70386 fax: (0474) 70455
46 rooms: Lire 80,000-120,000
Rates include breakfast & dinner
Open Dec 20 to Apr 10 and May 20 to Oct
Credit cards: none accepted
Beautiful mountain valley
Dolomites - near Austria
2 km SE of Sexton toward Moos
44 km E of Cortina, 116 km W of Bolzano

The Villa Igiea Grand Hotel is an oasis of blissful tranquility in the midst of the large and rather unattractive city of Palermo.   With all the fabulous archaeological sites and marvelous cathedrals in the area it is wonderful to have such a splendid hotel to "come home to" at night.   The approach to the Villa is not scenic, but from the moment you enter the gates you are in another world: a world of spacious lobbies, sweeping verandas, formal dining rooms, and generously sized, well furnished bedrooms with large modern bathrooms.   Many of the bedrooms have private balconies overlooking the gardens to the sea.   The hotel is called a villa, but it is much more like a small deluxe castle built right at the edge of the sea.   A lovely freeform swimming pool fits itself onto a ledge which overhangs the water. Next to the pool the hotel has its very own ancient Greek temple - now how many hotels can top that?   The most outstanding attributes of the hotel are the gardens which envelop the building in a nest of beautiful pines and masses of gorgeous flower beds intertwined with twisting pathways.   Altogether, a most delightful spot.

VILLA IGIEA GRAND HOTEL
Manager: Franco Arabia
Via Belmonte, 43 (Acquasanta)
90142 Palermo, Sicily, Italy
tel: (091) 543744   fax: (091) 547654
117 rooms: Lire 390,000
Open all year
Credit cards: all major
Swimming pool, tennis, sea front
Own small Greek temple by the sea
On northern coast of Sicily
U.S. Rep: Utell
Rep tel: 800-223-9868

The San Domenico Palace is a super deluxe hotel cleverly incorporated into what was formerly a Dominican monastery. Don't let the monastery bit deter you: absolutely no trace of a life of denial remains. In fact, this is one of the most super deluxe hotels in Italy, catering to your every whim. As you enter the building the lobby opens onto the core of the hotel, the beautiful arcaded Renaissance cloister. Around this inner courtyard the vaulted walkway is now glassed in, but filled with light. Leading off the courtyard are various lounges, writing rooms and game rooms. The dining room is a masterpiece: it has high backed wooden chairs, enormous arched windows and a paneled ceiling. The chapel has been converted into a bar. Throughout the hotel there are priceless antiques of a quality which would make a museum blush with pride. Many of the bedrooms look out to the beautiful bay of Taormina. In the rear of the hotel there is a lovely garden filled with gorgeous flowers and laced by pathways with small nooks where you can stop to soak in the splendid sea view. A swimming pool is squeezed into the property just as it drops down to the road below. There is no doubt that this is a MOST dramatic hotel.

SAN DOMENICO PALACE
Manager: Luigi Menta
Piazza San Domenico, 5
98039 Taormina, Sicily, Italy
tel: (0942) 23701 fax: (0942) 625506
100 rooms: Lire 610,000
Credit cards: all major
Swimming pool
On northern coast of Sicily
U.S. Rep: E & M Associates
Rep tel: 800-223-9832

Instead of being located in the ancient clifftop settlement of Taormina, the Villa Sant'Andrea is found in the village which clusters below. There is a cable car which can whisk you quickly back to Taormina for sightseeing or shopping. (The cable car is only a short block from the hotel so is very convenient.) If you are travelling with children the location is especially nice because the hotel is beautifully positioned at the end of a small swimming cove. In fact the property is built in levels which descend right to the beach where the hotel has its own private section for the guests. You enter the charming old villa from the street level where the reception desk is located. On a lower floor is the dining room which has an informal ambiance with white wicker furniture. The lounge maintains an "English country" look with sofas and chairs upholstered in cheerful floral prints which match the draperies. The bedrooms are simple but many have balconies with beautiful views across the small bay to the dramatic rocks jutting from the brilliant blue water. The hotel was originally built as a private residence for an English family in 1830 and it still maintains the ambiance of an English country estate.

VILLA SANT'ANDREA
Director: Francesco Moschella
98030 Taormina, Mazzaro
Sicily, Italy
tel: (0942) 23125 fax: (0942) 24838
67 rooms: Lire 340,000-360,000
Closed February
Credit cards: all major
Own private beach
On eastern coast of Sicily

If you would like to combine your sightseeing of Siena with a luxury resort, then the Certosa di Maggiano might be "just your cup of tea". This is an expensive hotel, but delightful and quite unique.   Outside, the hotel looks quite ordinary - just a wall facing the road - but when you step inside it is a fairyland.   It doesn't resemble a hotel in the slightest.   And it is no wonder: the hotel is built into the restored ruins of a 700-year-old Carthusian monastery.   As you enter the arcaded courtyard you can almost see the ghosts of priests, their dark robes flowing, silently walking beneath the vaulted roof of the cloisters.   On three sides of the courtyard are arranged the fourteen guest rooms, the lounges, the game rooms, the library, the bar and the exquisite dining room.   The fourth side of the courtyard is formed by a small church.   The guest rooms are spacious and pleasant but not outstanding in decor.   However, the public rooms are smashing, with antiques galore, and all of the finest quality.   Another bonus: there is a beautiful pool in the gardens which is never crowded since this is such a tiny hotel.   In fact, there are so few people around, that it truly is like being a guest in a private estate.

CERTOSA DI MAGGIANO
Manager: Anna Recordati
Via Certosa, 82/86
53100 Siena, Italy
tel: (577) 288180 fax: (0577) 288189
5 rooms: Lire 460,000
9 suites: Lire 620,000-730,000
Open all year
Credit cards: all major
Restaurant
Swimming pool and tennis
2 km E of Siena, near the Porta Romana gate

Although the Palazzo Ravizza is a much simpler hotel than we usually include in our guides, if you want to stay in Siena where you have the fun of walking to all the sights, this is the best choice.   There are many other more luxurious places to stay in the vicinity, but they are outside the city walls.   Even though the government has categorized it as a pensione, the Palazzo Ravizza definitely has some antique ambiance with the added bonus of being smack in the center of town.   A 17th-century mansion, the Palazzo Ravizza has belonged to the same family for nearly 200 years.   There are 30 bedrooms which all cost the same, even though they vary in their decor and location.   Some of the rooms are very basic, so be sure to ask for one of the best rooms - if possible, try to get one of the rooms with antique decor overlooking the garden.   The pretty back garden and terrace offer a panoramic view of the Tuscany hills, definitely one of the nicest aspects of this city hotel which fronts directly onto a commercial street.   Siena is sadly lacking in a choice of hotels, and the Palazzo Ravizza remains as one of the best choices for accommodation within the city walls.   The location is perfect: only a short walk from one of the most gorgeous cathedrals in Italy and only a stroll from the sensational fan-like plaza where the annual "running of the horses" takes place.

PENSIONE PALAZZO RAVIZZA
Manager: S. Iannone
Pian dei Mantellini, 34
53100 Siena, Italy
tel: (0577) 280462   fax: (0577) 271370
30 rooms: Lire 200,000-205,000
Rates include breakfast & dinner
Open all year
Credit cards: all major
Within the walled city of Siena

The Locanda dell'Amorosa makes a wonderful base for exploring the hill towns south of Florence.   It is very accessible since it is located in Sinalunga which is just a few minutes from the expressway between Rome and Florence.   From the Locanda dell'Amorosa it is an easy drive to such sightseeing delights as Siena, Pienza, Orvieto, Todi and Assisi.   However, it is not location alone which makes this hotel so perfect: there is far more.   Truly, the Locanda dell'Amorosa would be marvelous if there were nothing nearby - in fact, the hotel could be a destination in itself.   Actually, this is not a hotel: it is a tiny town a few miles south of Sinalunga. The approach to "town" is a road lined by a majestic row of cypress trees.   Park your car and enter the walls of the 14th-century medieval town where you are greeted by an enormous plaza with its own little church - exquisite inside with its soft pastels and its lovely fresco of the Madonna holding the Christ child.   To the right of the main entrance to the courtyard are the stables which have been converted to a beautiful restaurant whose massive beams, natural stone and brick walls are original and tastefully enhanced by arched windows, thick wrought iron fixtures and wooden tables.   The guest rooms, located in a separate building to the left of the main entrance, are tastefully appointed with a few antiques and matching bedspreads and draperies.   The rest of this tiny village spreads out behind the main square and the buildings are used for other purposes - including the production of wine.   A new swimming pool is scheduled for the summer of 1992.

LOCANDA DELL'AMOROSA
Manager: Carlo Citterio
53048 Sinalunga, Italy
tel: (0577) 679497 fax: (0577) 678216
15 rooms: Lire 320,000-440,000
Closed January 20 to February 28
Credit cards: AX DC VS
80 km S of Florence, 45 km E of Siena

What a sense of impending grandeur you experience as you wait for the giant metal gates of the Villa Cortine Palace to swing open. Once inside the road winds and curves impressively past fountains and statues, flower gardens and mighty trees until you reach the summit where the Villa Cortine Palace reigns. This beautifully situated villa has been expanded so that the original wing now boasts a new section which appears to have more than doubled the size of the original castle. Some of the remodeling has a "too modern" feel: one rather wishes that perhaps more of an "old-world" ambiance could have been preserved. However, in the old section of the villa, which is to the left as you enter the lobby, the rooms still maintain their grandeur with incredibly ornate furniture, soaring ceilings and stunning paintings. Upstairs the guest rooms are large and are decorated with color coordinated drapes, chairs and bedspreads. What leaves absolutely nothing to be improved upon are the gardens - what a gorgeous sight. In fact, they are absolutely awe-inspiring. The villa is surrounded by graveled walkways which wind in and out amongst the fountains, ponds, statues, and glorious rose gardens, all overlooking the lovely lake.

VILLA CORTINE PALACE HOTEL
25019 Sirmione, Italy
tel: (030) 916021 fax: (030) 916390
55 rooms: Lire 330,000-400,000
2 suites: Lire 700,000-820,000
Minimum stay 3 days
Open April to November
Credit cards: all major
Swimming pool, tennis, lake pier
Park setting - overlooks Lake Garda
127 km E of Milan, 35 km W of Verona

The Grand Hotel Excelsior Vittoria has a superb location high on the cliff overlooking the port and bay of Sorrento and surrounded by an orange grove and park of about four acres with a swimming pool.   The hotel is a grand old villa with a real "old-world" atmosphere, entered through a formal gate which is just a short stroll from the center of town.   The furnishings, for the most part, continue the antique mood.   The Excelsior Vittoria is a good place to splurge and reserve one of the superior rooms with a view of the sea.   The ceilings in some of the reception rooms and in the marvelous airy dining room have gorgeous frescoed designs.   The terraces and gardens surrounding the hotel offer wonderful views, as do the bedrooms which face the bay.   When we first saw the Grand Hotel Excelsior Vittoria there was a gracious, though faded, elegance to the hotel giving it a slightly "worn" look.   However, this magnificent villa has since been lovingly restored under the guidance of Lidia Fiorentino, the owner's wife, carefully retaining the unique turn-of-the-century mood.   Staying here will certainly delight anyone who loves the feeling of reliving the grandeur of days gone by in a villa by the sea.

GRAND HOTEL EXCELSIOR VITTORIA
Owner: Fiorentino Family
Piazza Torquato Tasso, 34
80067 Sorrento, Italy
tel: (081) 8071044 fax: (081) 8771206
125 rooms: Lire 277,000-340,000
Suites: to Lire 750,000
Open all year
Credit cards: all major
Swimming pool, elevator to harbor
48 km S of Naples, 50 km N of Salerno
U.S. Rep: Utell International
Rep tel: 800-223-9868

The road to the Pensione Stefaner winds up a tiny mountain valley in the heart of the Dolomites. The road is spectacular, but extremely narrow, and twists like a snake around blind curves whose roadside mirrors are a necessity, not an optional precaution. As we rounded the last curve before Tiers the valley opened up and there spread before us a sweeping vista of majestically soaring mountains. Across soft green meadows painted with wildflowers and dotted with tiny farm chalets rose an incredible saw-toothed range of gigantic peaks. Suddenly the journey seemed worth the effort for the scenery alone even if the Pensione Stefaner proved to be a disaster. Luckily, though, the Pensione Stefaner is very nice. The outside is especially attractive - a chalet with flower-laden balconies. Inside, the inn is a bit too "fussy" for my taste, but the valley is so spectacular that I am sure you will be spending most of your time on the beautiful walking trails which lace the valley. The Pensione Stefaner has some antiques scattered throughout for accents, but the furniture is new. The bedrooms are light and airy and many have balconies. Although there was no one who spoke English when I was there, friendliness prevailed. In fact, there was even a gentle, lazy German Shepherd lounging in the lobby offering a friendly welcome. Note: Tiers is called Tires on some maps.

PENSIONE STEFANER
Owner: Villgrattner Family
39050 Tiers (Tires), Italy
tel: (0471) 642175
15 rooms: Lire 120,000
Rate includes breakfast & dinner
Closed mid-November to mid-December
Credit cards: none accepted
New chalet-style inn
NE Italy in Dolomites
17 km E of Bolzano, 3 km E of Stefaner

Le Tre Vaselle is a very sophisticated inn located in the small wine town of Torgiano which is very near Assisi. The decor of the hotel is one of a lovely country manor. The owners are the Lungarotti family, famous for their production of superb wines: Mr. Lungarotti owns all of the vineyards around Torgiano for as far as the eye can see. The hotel probably evolved to fill the need for a place for business associates and friends to stay when visiting the vineyards. The accommodations are extremely comfortable and have all the amenities of a large city hotel. The most amazing aspect of Le Tre Vaselle is that it has stunning conference rooms furnished in antiques with intimate adjacent dining rooms. The Lungarotti family has thought of everything: to keep the wives happy while their husbands are in meetings, the hotel schedules cooking classes in one of the most professional kitchens I have ever seen. The Lungarottis also have a private wine museum which would be a masterpiece anywhere in the world. Not only do they have an incredible and comprehensive collection of anything pertaining to wine throughout the ages, but the display is a work of art. The museum alone would be worth a detour to Le Tre Vaselle.

LE TRE VASELLE
Owner: Lungarotti Family
Via Garibaldi, 48
06089 Torgiano, Italy
tel: (075) 982447 fax: (075) 985214
48 rooms: Lire 280,000-390,000
Ooen all year
Credit cards: AX DC VS
27 km SW of Assisi, 158 km N of Rome
Superb wine museum

The Baia Paraelios is an absolutely delightful hotel tucked onto the spur of land that juts from the toe of Italy near the ancient port of Tropea. The hotel is actually a resort which follows the contours of the hillside from the highway down to the beach. The reception office is located at the top of the hill and the mood is set from the moment you register. The small office is tastefully decorated with plants and charming old prints on the walls and the personnel in the office are gracious and warm in their welcome. The rooms are all bungalows which are artfully terraced down the hill to capture the best view possible from each. Midway down is a lovely pool. At beach level is a beautiful dining room and a comfortable, inviting lounge. The bungalows each have one or more bedrooms, a sitting room and a deck or patio. The decor is simple but in excellent taste with tiled floors and earth tones used throughout. One of the most beautiful white sand beaches I saw in Italy stretches invitingly in front of the complex. The Baia Paraelios makes a nice stop along your route south. Not only will you have the benefit of a lovely break in your travels, but also the nearby ancient town of Tropea, which hangs on the cliffs above a beautiful bay, is fun to explore.

BAIA PARAELIOS
Owner: Adolfo Salabe
88035 Parghelia
Tropea, Italy
tel: (0963) 600300 fax: (0963) 600074
70 bungalows: Lire 580,000-665,000
Rates include 3 meals a day
Open May 10 through September
Pool, tennis, gorgeous beach
Southern Italy - near tip of toe
420 km S of Naples, 5 km N of Tropea

Susan and John Abbot hail from the East Coast of the United States, but they have lived in Italy for over 20 years, and it is now "home" to them. When they saw the Castello di Polgeto, it was love at first sight, and, according to John, they bought it in 20 minutes. I can certainly understand why. The castle is idyllically perched on a hillside with blissful vistas of vineyards, olive groves, green meadows and wooded hills - Umbria at its finest. When they purchased it, the castle was practically a shell: they had to install bathrooms, build proper roofs, add walls, tile the floors, wire for adequate electricity, plant artistic landscaping and on and on. It has been years of work, but John is both an artist and architect so it has all pulled together like a dream. Six self-catering apartments, individually decorated using native rustic materials, choice country antiques and simple fabrics, are artfully integrated with modern furniture and abstract paintings. A lovely pool is tucked into a secluded terrace below the castle. By the time you arrive, Susan and John might have completed their latest addition, a wonderful suite in the ancient tower. Note: The closest town to the Castello di Polgeto on the Hallwag map is Umbertide.

CASTELLO DI POLGETO
Owners: Susan & John Abbot
06019 Umbertide-Polgeto, Italy
tel: (075) 9413719 fax: (075) 9413719
6 apartments: 400-465 English pounds per week
3 night minimum, week stays preferred
Reservations only through Harrison-Stanton/London
tel: UK (071) 7365094 fax: UK (071) 3842327
Credit cards: none accepted
No restaurant, apartments self-catering
No children under age 16
30 km N of Perugia, 4 km SW of Umbertide

The Bewallerhof, an appealing inn tucked into a remote valley in the Dolomites, has a fabulous setting: a meadow of green velvet stretching out in front to a far vista of beautiful mountain peaks, spectacular giant walls of granite forming the backdrop, wildflowers in the fields, cows munching grass in the distance. The hotel, built upon the site of an old farmhouse, offers walking trails spider-webbing out in every direction, pleasant decor, good food, and a large, sunny terrace. (Note: We had a complaint that a reservation was not honored - please let us know if you have any problems). Even with excellent maps, the inn is extremely tricky to find. An added confusion is that each of the towns has two names. But finding it is half the fun: here are a few hints. The Bewallerhof is located in the Val d'Ega between the towns of Eggen (Ega) and Obereggen (San Floriano). If coming from Bolzano head southeast through the Val d'Ega for approximately 16 kilometers watching for the turn to the right for Obereggen. If you arrive at Nova Levante (Welschnofen) you have gone too far. If coming from Cortina, follow the "Old Dolomite Road" west from Cortina watching carefully for the turnoff toward Nova Levante. When you reach Nova Levante it is only about 4 kilometers until you reach the road to the left for Obereggen. Note: The closest town on the Hallwag map is Ega - the index says *Ega* but what shows on the map is Val d'Ega.

HOTEL BEWALLERHOF
Proprietor: Eisath Family
39050 Obereggen (San Floriano)
Val d'Ega, Italy
tel: (0471) 615729
22 rooms: Lire 140,000
Rate include breakfast & dinner
Open June 25 to Oct 20 and Dec 20 to Apr 15
Credit cards: none accepted
25 km SE of Bolzano, 3 km S of Nova Levante

The Gasthof Obereggen, located in the Val d'Ega (Ega Valley) is very simple, but quite wonderful.   The inn is situated on the side of a hill overlooking a gorgeous mountain valley in one of the most beautiful mountain regions of northeastern Italy.   The town of Obereggen is a ski resort and the lift is just a few minutes' walk away.   From the sun-drenched deck which extends generously out from the hotel, there is an absolutely glorious vista across the green meadows to the mountains. Behind the hotel even more majestic mountains poke their jagged peaks into the sky.   Inside there is a cozy dining room.   Mr. Pichler must be a hunter, for trophies line the walls, and there is a typical tiled stove against one wall to keep the room toasty on a cold day.   The inn has 12 bedrooms - those on the second floor open out onto lovely view-balconies.   The greatest asset of this inn, and the real reason for its inclusion, is Mrs. Pichler: she is very special - running her little inn with such a warmth and gaiety that just being in the same room with her is fun. Mrs. Pichler speaks no English, but her hospitality crosses all language barriers, and her bountiful, delicious "home style" cooking speaks to all who love to eat. Note: Obereggen is almost impossible to find on any map, although the Val d'Ega is usually indicated - please see general driving instructions given under the Hotel Bewallerhof (page 232).   Note: The closest town on the Hallwag map is Ega (Ega is called San Floriano on some maps).

GASTHOF OBEREGGEN
Owner: Pichler Family
39050 Obereggen (San Floriano)
Val d'Ega, Italy
tel: (0471) 615722
12 rooms: Lire 120,000
Rates include breakfast & dinner
Credit cards: none accepted
25 km SE of Bolzano, 3 km S of Nova Levante

The Stella d'Italia is located in San Mamete, a tiny, picturesque village nestled along the northern shore of Lake Lugano, just a few minutes' drive from the Swiss border.   The hotel (which has been in the Ortelli family for three generations) makes an excellent choice for a moderately priced lakefront hotel.   Mario Ortelli, an extremely cordial host, showed us throughout the hotel which has two adjoining wings, one quite old and the other a new addition.   My choice for accommodation would be in the original part which has more "old-world" ambiance - the rooms I saw here were very pleasant with large French windows opening onto miniature balconies capturing views of the lake.   The lounges and dining room have a few antique accents, but basically have a modern ambiance.   The nicest feature of the hotel is the superb little lakefront garden - in summer this is where all the guests "live".   Green lawn, fragrant flowers, lacy trees, and a romantic vine-covered trellised dining area make this an ideal spot for whiling away the hours.   Steps lead down to a small pier from which guests can swim.   The ferry dock for picking up and dropping off passengers is adjacent to the hotel.   Another interesting feature for golf enthusiasts is that there are several golf courses within an easy drive from the hotel - one of these (near the town of Grandola) is one of the oldest in Italy.

STELLA D'ITALIA
Owner: Mario Ortelli
San Mamete
22010 Valsolda
Lake Lugano, Italy
tel: (0344) 68139 fax: (0344) 68729
36 rooms: Lire 95,000-105,000
Open April through September
Credit cards: all major
Lakefront hotel, swimming pier
8 km E of Lugano, 100 km N of Milan

The Pensione Accademia is enchanting - a fairytale villa with delightful gardens, romantic canal-side location, and cozy antique-filled interior. The hotel has a fabulous setting on an oasis of land almost looped by canals. In front is a beautiful, completely enclosed, "secret" garden whose walls are so heavily draped with vines that it is not until you discover black iron gates that you see steps leading down to the villa's own gondola landing. As you leave the garden and enter the wisteria-covered palazzo, the magic continues with family heirlooms adorning the spacious rooms where sunlight filters through large windows. A staircase leads upstairs where some of the guest rooms are located in the original villa and others, connected by a hallway, in a portion of the hotel borrowed from an adjacent building. No two of the guest rooms are alike, none are "decorator perfect" - they are like guest rooms in a private home. Some of those in the front have canal views but are noisier than those looking over the garden. The only hitch to this picture of perfection is that your chances are slim of snaring a room in this romantic hideaway - the hotel is so special that loyal guests reserve "their" own favorite room for the following year as they leave. Spring and fall are most heavily booked - your chances are better in July and August and the prices are even a little lower. Since we last visited the Pensione Accademia, it has come under new management. We will be eager to hear readers' comments.

PENSIONE ACCADEMIA
Manager: Giovnna Salmaso
Dorsoduro 1058
3123 Venice, Italy
tel: (041) 5237846   fax: (041) 5239152
26 rooms: Lire 196,000
Open all year
Credit cards: all major
Near the Accademia boat stop

Hotel Descriptions　　　235

The Agli Alboretti Hotel is conveniently located just steps from the Accademia boat landing.   Although only a two star hotel, it has more charm than many others charging much higher prices.   But it is not price alone that makes the hotel appealing: there is a cozy ambiance from the moment you step into the intimate lobby, paneled with dark mellowed wood and decorated with some attractive prints on the walls and a perky ship model in the window.   At the front desk will be either Dina Linguerri or her daughter Anna.   I did not meet Anna, but her mother is most gracious and speaks excellent English.   Beyond the reception area is a small lounge and then one of the very nicest features of the hotel - a tranquil garden sheltered by an overhanging trellis which in summer is completely covered by vines - a welcome, cool oasis after a day of sightseeing.   White wrought iron tables and chairs are set for morning breakfast, afternoon tea, or summer evening dinner. The guest rooms vary in size, but all have a private bath or shower.   Be sure to request a guest room with a *bath tub* because the showers are the type without a separate enclosure.   Whichever room you have, however, it should be quiet since the hotel is tucked onto a peaceful square.   Note: There is a restaurant which serves dinner every night except Wednesday.

AGLI ALBORETTI HOTEL
Owners: Dina & Anna Linguerri
Dorsoduro 882-884
30123 Venice, Italy
tel: (041) 5230058 fax: (041) 5210158
19 rooms: Lire 127,000
Open all year
Credit cards: all major
Simple hotel, restaurant closed Wednesday
Near the Accademia boat stop

The Hotel Flora is reached down a tiny lane, just off one of the main walkways to St Mark's Square: a secluded hideaway, protected from the bustle of the city yet conveniently close to all the action.   At the end of the tiny alley the doors open into a small lobby, beyond which is an enchanting small garden, an oasis of serenity with white wrought iron tables and chairs surrounding a gently tinkling fountain. Potted plants, small trees and lacy vines complete the idyllic scene.   The hotel encloses the garden on three sides: doors open to the right to a dear little bar and the breakfast room.   The lounges are Victorian in mood with dark furniture.   The bedrooms vary in their size and decor, but all are fancy and have ornate, antique furnishings.   Victorian-style wallpaper covers many of the walls.   The ambiance is a bit fussy, but with a definite old world atmosphere.   There is no restaurant at the hotel, which is absolutely no problem since Venice abounds with wonderful places to dine.   Breakfast, of course, is served to guests.   Signor Romanelli, who owns this small hotel, personally sees that his guests are well taken care of.   The Hotel Flora is a favorite of many travellers to Venice.   Although it is a relatively simple hotel and would not appeal to those looking for deluxe accommodations, it is a real find for those who want a relatively inexpensive place to stay in the heart of Venice.

HOTEL FLORA
Owner: Alex Romanelli
Calle larga 22 Marzo, 2283/a
30124 Venice, Italy
tel: (041) 5205844   fax: (041) 5228217
44 rooms: Lire 224,000 (with air conditioning)
Open February to November 20
Credit cards: all major
No restaurant - breakfast only
3-minute walk from St Mark's Square
U.S. Rep: JDL 800-366-1510

If you love opulent elegance, and if cost is of no consequence to you, the Gritti Palace is an excellent choice for your hotel in Venice. The location is marvelous - just a short walk from St Mark's Square yet far enough removed to miss the city's noise and summer mob of tourists. In fact, with careful planning, you can be entirely insulated in a private and very special world from the moment you arrive until you reluctantly depart. If you take a private motor launch from the airport or the Piazza Roma, you can descend stylishly at the deluxe little private pier in front of the hotel where porters will be waiting to whisk you to your room to be pampered and spoiled. All at a price, of course. The Gritti Palace is expensive, very expensive. But then what would you expect when staying in the 15th-century palace of the immensely wealthy Venetian Doge, Andrea Gritti. The Gritti Palace has a charming terrace on the bank of the Grand Canal where you dine in splendor and watch the constant stream of boat traffic. The lobby and lounge areas open off the terrace and are grandly decorated with antiques. The bedrooms are large and very fancy in decor, and those that face the canal are presented with a 24-hour show.

HOTEL GRITTI PALACE
Manager: Vincenzo Finizzola
Campo S. Maria del Giglio, 2467
30124 Venice, Italy
tel: (041) 794611   fax: (041) 5200942
99 rooms: Lire 609,280-728,280
Open all year
Credit cards: all major
Exquisite old palace
Near St Mark's Square
U.S. Rep: CIGA Hotels
Rep tel: 800-221-2340

The Hotel La Fenice et Des Artistes, although not inexpensive, costs less than many other hotels which do not offer nearly its charm.   The lobby is small, but seems spacious since there are two small garden patios which open from it.   Here guests sit in the late afternoon for a cup of tea or an aperitif before dinner.   Doors to the right lead to a club-like lounge and an intimate bar.   The reception area is a triangle which connects the original building on the right with a newer wing on the left.   Both sections are nice, although in summer only the newer wing offers the option of air conditioning, which can be very welcome on a hot day (there is an additional charge for air conditioned rooms.)   The bedrooms are not large, but adequate, and color coordinated with a different wallpaper in each room setting the theme.   Breakfast is the only meal served, but this is almost a blessing since within a few blocks there is a fabulous choice of appealing places to dine.   The fascinating La Fenice Theater, one of the oldest and most beautiful theaters in Europe, is just around the corner - most conveniently located for music lovers.   Note: we have received some complaints about the hotel's management not being overly gracious and that a refurbishing of the rooms is needed.   We will appreciate any feedback - we've always liked this hotel.

HOTEL LA FENICE ET DES ARTISTES
Manager: Dante Appollonio
Campiello de la Fenice, S. Marco 1936
30124 Venice, Italy
tel: (041) 5232333   fax: (041) 5203721
75 rooms: Lire 208,000
Open all year
Credit cards: MC VS
Near La Fenice Theatre

Although La Residenza, with its arched windows, lacy detailing, and columned balcony, is a brilliant example of the finest 15th-century Venetian architecture, I was at first a bit half-hearted in my enthusiasm due to the somewhat dilapidated condition of the small plaza it faces.   When I visited the hotel, the massive door was locked and I started to turn away until I discovered a discreetly camouflaged small button incorporated into a brass lion ornament to the left of the door.   This I rang and the owner, Franco Tagliapietra, leaned out the window and instructed me in Italian to push open the door when he released the lock.   How glad I was that I had persevered.   After entering the door and climbing up a flight of stairs, I was magically surrounded by a beautiful, museum-quality room with walls and ceiling adorned with intricate plaster designs.   The softly toned walls and the marble floor were enhanced by dark wooden furniture.   All of the bedrooms have a private bath and are accented with fine antiques.   You might have a problem booking this small hotel, since no one seems to speak English.   However, perhaps use the Italian form letter in the back of this guide or get an Italian speaking friend to call for you.   It is no wonder the palace is so splendid - it was the residence of the Gritti family, a most prestigious name in Venice.   Note: Readers have written that their deposits were not returned when they had to cancel reservations.

LA RESIDENZA
Owner: Franco Tagliapietra
Campo Bandiera e Moro
30122 Venice, Italy
tel: (041) 5285315   fax: (041) 5238859
15 rooms: Lire 130,000
Closed February 8-20
Credit cards: AX VS
Beautiful 15th-century palace
Located 10-minute walk from St Mark's Square

At first glance the exterior of the Pensione Seguso appears quite bland: a rather boxy affair without much of the elaborate architectural enhancements so frequently evident in Venice. However, the inside of the pensione radiates warmth and charm with Oriental rugs setting off antique furniture and heirloom silver service. The hotel is located on the "left bank" of Venice - across the Grand Canal from the heart of the tourist area, about a 15-minute walk to St Mark's Square (or only a few minutes by ferry from the Accademia boat stop). For several generations the hotel has been in the Seguso family who provide a homelike ambiance for the guest who does not demand luxury. In front there is a miniature terrace harboring a few tables set under umbrellas. Several of the bedrooms have views of the canal (although these rooms are the noisiest due to the canal traffic). Remember this is a simple pension, most of the rooms share a bathroom: if you are looking for the amenities offered by a hotel, the Pensione Seguso would not be for you. But, the most pleasant surprise is that the value-conscious tourist can stay at the Pensione Seguso with breakfast and dinner included for what the price of a room alone would cost for most hotels in Venice. Note: Although a small pensione, the Seguso has an elevator - handy if you have a problem with stairs.

PENSIONE SEGUSO
Owner: Seguso Family
Grand Canal Zattere, 779
30123 Venice, Italy
tel: (041) 5222340   fax: (041) 5222340
36 rooms: Lire 179,000-211,500
Rates include breakfast & dinner
Credit cards: none accepted
10-minute walk from the Accademia boat stop

The Casa Frollo, located on Giudecca Island across from St Mark's Square, is a real gem: a moderately-priced oasis just minutes from the heart of Venice.   There is constant ferry service to and from the island so the distance is not a problem (actually the boat ride is quite fun).   Once you arrive at Giudecca (getting off at the Riva degli Schiavoni dock), walk to your right and you will see the Casa Frollo, an old villa across the street from the water.   You enter through huge doors and then climb the stairs to your right to bring you into an enormous reception - all-purpose room.   When I first visited the Casa Frollo, is was run by Flora Soldan, but now her son, Marino has taken over the management.   My heart was won the moment I stepped into the room which is brimming with priceless antiques and was enveloped by its awesome size.   The room runs the length of the building and the front windows (where tables are set for breakfast and drinks) open onto a sensational view of Venice.   The bedrooms vary in decor but are spacious and many with antiques.   The rear windows open onto a lazy, lush garden.   For those on a tight budget, there are some rooms without baths.   For splurges, request a bath and a view of Venice.

CASA FROLLO
Manager: Marino Soldan
Giudecca, 50
30133 Venice, Italy
tel: (041) 5222723   fax: (041) 5206203
26 rooms: Lire 100,000-140,000
Open March 18 to November 21
Credit cards: none accepted
17th-century palace
Splendid view of St Mark's Square
On Giudecca Island

The Hotel Cipriani was founded by the late Giuseppe Cipriani, who during his lifetime became almost a legend in Venice.   This beloved man, who founded the internationally famous Harry's Bar in Venice, had a dream of building a fabulous hotel within easy reach of St Mark's Square and yet far enough away to guarantee seclusion and peace.   He bought three acres on the island of Giudecca and with the financial assistance of some of his prestigious friends, such as Princess Briget of Prussia and the Earl of Iveagh (head of the Guinness brewing company in Dublin), he accomplished his dream - an elegant Venetian palace-style hotel.   The Cipriani is the perfect hotel for those of you who *must* have a pool, for it is the only hotel with a pool in Venice.   And what a pool - it is Olympic size and surrounded by beautiful gardens.   The splendor continues inside where the lounges are tastefully decorated in whites and beiges and the bedrooms are large and elegant.   You truly have the best of all worlds at the Cipriani - you are at a superior resort yet only minutes from the heart of Venice in the private launch which waits to whisk you, any time of the day or night, to St Mark's Square.   Note: Since our last visit, 9 super deluxe apartments have opened in the renovated *Palazzo Vendramin*, adjacent to the hotel.   We have not yet been able to inspect this new addition, but from the pictures we have seen, they are absolutely gorgeous.

HOTEL CIPRIANI
Manager: Dr. Natale Rusconi
Isola della Giudecca, 10
30123 Venice, Italy
tel: (041) 5207744   fax: (041) 5203930
105 rooms: Lire 650,000-2,800,000
Open March to November
Credit cards: all major
Swimming pool, tennis court, yacht harbor
On Giudecca Island

If the idea of being close to Venice and yet near a beach and casino appeals to you, then perhaps you should consider a hotel located on the Lido, a small island opposite St Mark's Square.   A fifteen-minute boat ride and a short taxi trip brings you to the Albergo Quattro Fontane, a charming inn which reminds me more of a French country home than an Italian villa.   It has a white stuccoed exterior with gabled roof, green shutters, and vines creeping both over the door and around some of the small balconies.   To the left of the main building is a lovely courtyard whose privacy is established by another wing of the hotel giving the garden a cozy, "walled in" effect.   Inside the hotel there is an ambiance of a country home with antiques cleverly used throughout the lounges.   The beach is only a short distance away and the Albergo Quattro Fontane can make arrangements for you to reserve a private beach cabana when you arrive at the inn.   The cost per day will vary, depending both upon the location and the comparative luxury of the cabana you choose.   The beach is wide and the water inviting and clear, although the sand is not as fine and white as we have seen on some of the beaches in southern Italy.   Still, it is quite an experience just to sample the interesting hierarchy of the Italian beach system.

ALBERGO QUATTRO FONTANE
Via 4 Fontane
30126 Lido of Venice
Venice, Italy
tel: (041) 5260227 fax: (041) 5260726
68 rooms: Lire 250,000-280,000
Open end of April to October 1
Credit cards: AX VS
Recently all the rooms have been air conditioned
Near casino, beach, tennis
On the Lido, across from Venice

The tiny island of Torcello is located about fifty minutes from Venice by boat. This lovely, sleepy little island is usually considered a short stop for the tour boats as they ply their way among the maze of little islands surrounding Venice. But, for those who want to linger on Torcello, where they can be close to Venice yet feel out in the country, there is a deluxe inn which is owned by the Cipriani family. This small inn, the Locanda Cipriani, is well known to knowledgeable gourmets as a fantastic restaurant. Many arrive every day from Venice just to dine, and depart never knowing that upstairs this restaurant also has guest rooms. The inn is very simple, much more like a small farmhouse than a deluxe hotel. Inside there is a rustic, cozy dining room and outside a beautiful dining terrace surrounded by gardens brilliant in summer with all varieties of flowers. There are only a few bedrooms which are all suites. Breakfast and dinner are included in the room rate. This is an expensive inn, but an elegant hideaway for relaxing and dining royally in a beautiful country setting. Many famous guests have already discovered this oasis - including Hemingway, who came here to write. I think you will share his belief that the Locanda Cipriani Torcello is a very special place.

LOCANDA CIPRIANI TORCELLO
Owner: Cipriani Family
Manager: Bonifacio Brass (son)
30012 Isola Torcello
Venice, Italy
tel: (041) 730150 fax: (041) 735433
5 suites: Lire 520,000
Rate includes breakfast & dinner
Open mid-March to mid-November
Credit cards: AX DC VS
Luxury inn on quiet little island
Reached by boat from Venice

The Hotel due Torri is not a cozy little inn, but it has its own style.   You enter into an enormous central inner court which is almost like a football field - a football field with a floor of large rust and cream colored tile that looks like a chessboard. Encircling the room are columns supporting arches which form an arcade.   The ceiling is covered with brilliant paintings. Bright green and red comfortable lounge chairs form small groupings for conversation.   After the initial impact, the room begins to "grow on you", especially when you read the history and realize that in the 14th Century the Lords of Verona used this building as their official guest house. The bedrooms are even more unusual than the lobby.   Each has genuine antique furniture meticulously collected to maintain authenticity.   Each of the bedrooms has a different decor: most feature very ornate furnishings.   Some of the rooms are Louis XVI style, others Greek-Roman, others Charles X period, others English. But all have real antiques.   To make this choice of rooms even more fun, there is a set of slides in the lobby where you can look at the pictures of the various rooms and pick out one that especially suits your mood.   Note: There is now an elegant new restaurant at Hotel due Torri called All 'Aquila.

HOTEL DUE TORRI
Owner: Enrico Wallner
Manager: R. Giavarini
Piazza San Anastasia, 4
37100 Verona, Italy
tel: (045) 595044   fax: (045) 8004130
96 rooms: Lire 396,000-540,000
Open all year
Credit cards: all major
Authentic antiques used throughout
In the heart of Verona

The entrance to the Hotel Victoria is starkly modern - almost with a museum-like quality. The white walls, white ceiling, white floors, and an enormous skylight are softened by the green plants. At first glance I was disappointed since I had heard so many glowing reports of the merits of this small hotel. However, the mood begins to change as you enter the reception area with its Oriental carpets and, by the time you arrive in the lounge area, the feeling is definitely moving toward an antique ambiance with the original heavy ancient wooden beams and one of the original stone walls exposed, leather chairs, and some lovely antique tables. The bedrooms are extremely modern and beautifully functional with good reading lights, comfortable chairs, and excellent bathrooms. The Victoria actually dates back centuries and the new hotel is built within the shell of an ancient building. The architect even incorporated some of the archaeologically interesting finds of the site into a museum in the basement level. When the hotel is not full and all of the dining room tables are not needed, special "windows" open up on the floor of the restaurant and the museum below is lit so that you can study the artifacts as you dine.

HOTEL VICTORIA
Manager: Luciano Tamburini
Via Adua, 6
37121 Verona, Italy
tel: (045) 590566 fax: (045) 590155
46 rooms: Lire 213,000-235,000
Open all year
Credit cards: AX DC VS
In the heart of Verona

The Hotel Turm belongs to the Romantik Hotel Chain. Just being a member of this exclusive "club" indicates the hotel is pretty special because to belong the inn must have the owner personally involved in the management and the interior must have an antique ambiance. The Hotel Turm is no exception. There is an especially attractive little dining room with vaulted whitewashed ceilings and chalet-style rustic wooden furniture. There are a few antiques in the hallways and lounges. The bedrooms are simple, but very pleasant, with light pine furniture and fluffy down comforters on the beds. There is a swimming pool on the terrace where one can swim or lounge while gazing out to the little town and the mountains beyond. There is even a small indoor pool. The Hotel Turm dates back to the 13th Century and Mr. Pramstrahler takes great care to maintain touches of the "old-world" charm by interspersing antique chests, cradles, chairs and ancient artifacts. Note: Vols is called Fie on some maps.

ROMANTIK HOTEL TURM
Owner: Pramstrahler Family
Fie Allo Schiliar
1-39050 Vols am Schlern
Sudtirol, Italy
tel: (0471) 725014 fax: (0471) 725474
24 rooms: Lire 120,000-170,000
Closed November 15 to December 20
Credit cards: MC VS
Indoor and outdoor pools
16 km E of Bolzano, 7 km S of Siusi (Seis)
U.S. Rep: Romantik Hotel
Rep tel: 800-826-0015

Inn Discoveries from Our Readers

Many of the hotels newly featured in this edition are those you recommended to us and which we inspected and agreed wholeheartedly with your appraisal.   However, there were some we never had the opportunity to see.   We have a firm policy never to feature any hotel, no matter how perfect it sounds, until we have made a personal inspection.   This seemed a waste of some excellent "tips", so, to solve this dilemma, the following section features places to stay that you have shared with us, but which we have not yet had the opportunity to visit.   Thank you for your discoveries.

ACQUAFREDDA (MARATEA)   HOTEL VILLA CHETA ELITE

Hotel Villa Cheta Elite, Strada Statale, Acquafredda, 85041 Potenza, Italy; Owners: Marisa and Lamberto Aquadro; tel: (0973) 878134, fax: (0973) 878134; Open April - September; 18 rooms: Lire 98,000-135,000.

We had targeted the Hotel Villa Cheta Elite as a potential "to see" for this edition, but our research did not take us to the south of Italy.   We have seen pictures and received rave reviews of this small hotel located in one of our favorite coastal regions on the western coast of southern Italy and it sounds like a real winner. The hotel overlooks the sea and meals are served when the weather is balmy outside on the terrace.   The food is supposed to be good, featuring fish Specialties. One reader (of Italian heritage) who stayed at the Hotel Villa Cheta Elite wrote: "From an Italian's point of view, the hotel is absolutely delightful.   The handsome owners are warm and gracious, and, although they speak no English, are excellent hosts to all the guests."   We are eager to try out the hotel ourselves - we definitely will on our next trip to Italy.

BOLOGNA   HOTEL OROLOGIO

Hotel Orologio, Manager: Mauro Orsi, Via IV Novembre, 10, 40123 Bologna, Italy, tel: (051) 231253, fax: (051) 360553, 29 rooms: Lire 154,000-175,000

At the time of our last research trip to Italy we were disappointed that the beautifully located Hotel Orologio was closed for renovations, but now we hear it is open as a three star hotel. "This hotel is wonderfully located just on Piazza Maggiore, in front of Palazzo Comunale. Most of the rooms have a delightful view of the Piazza and the principal monuments. It is ideal for the shopping in the historical center." *Recommended by Paolo Orsi, Hotel Corona d'Oro, Bologna.*

LUCCA   VILLA RINASCIMENTO

Villa Rinascimento, Carla and Vincenzo Zaffora, 55058 Maria del Giudice, Lucca, Italy; tel: (0583) 370238 or (0583) 378201; 15 rooms with bath at Lire 90,000; *Recommended by Marilyn and Charles Coffaro, Harrison, Ohio.*

Situated only 9 kilometers from Lucca, a marvelous city completely enclosed by walls, is a new recommendation that we are especially pleased to pass on to you since there are so few places in the area to stay. "While on a trip to Italy last month we discovered the Villa Rinascimento which we believe meets your standards. We stayed two nights and it was wonderful. Carla (she's Dutch) and Fincenzo have spent 7 years restoring the building. Carla speaks English, German and French along with Italian. There is a swimming pool and lovely garden. It is very peaceful and a great spot for visiting Lucca and Pisa. They are constantly improving the surrounding green area around the Villa. It is truly a great bargain".

MASSA COZZILE   VILLA PASQUINI

Villa Pasquini, Family Innocenti, Via Vacchereccia, 56, Montecatini - Massa Cozzile - PT, Italy; tel: (0572) 72205; Lire 96,000 *Recommended by Anna LaPorta-Balsamo, Brooklyn, New York*

"We found the fantastic Villa Pasquini (remodeled in 1990) near Montecatini, 20 minutes from Florence.   You are greeted by Mr. Innocenti and his family who are dedicated to making your stay a happy one.   The dining room overlooks the gorgeous mountains and farms and groves.   The bedrooms are really too beautiful to be real.   I could go on and one, but I must end by telling you about the gourmet meals of classic Tuscan food served nightly in an elegant atmosphere in the main dining room with classical music accenting the already perfect evening.   We loved the Villa Pasquini so much that we ended up staying a week and going each day by bus to Florence."   Anna sent a brochure and photographs.   The Villa Pasquini does indeed look fabulous.   It will be a "must see" on our next trip to Italy

SORRENTO   IMPERIAL TRAMONTANO HOTEL

Imperial Tramontano Hotel, via Vittorio Veneto, 80067 Sorrento, Italy; tel: (081) 878 1940, fax: (091) 8072344; 109 rooms: Lire 275,000; Open April - October; *Recommended by Debby Lumkes.*

"You may want to check out the Imperial Tramontano Hotel in Sorrento.   We had a room that had a sitting room, bedroom and huge bathroom with two balconies, one in the sitting room and one in the bedroom, overlooking the harbor, Capri and Vesuvius.   The facilities are wonderful, the lobby is beautiful and there is greenery surrounding the entrance to the establishment."

Hotel Pausania, Dorso Duro, 2824, Venice 30100, Italy; tel: (041) 5222083; 26 rooms: Lire 240,000; *Anonymous, Hillsborough, California*

"I have a hotel for you in Venice, an absolutely perfect one, Hotel Pausania. One takes the #11 Ca'Rezzonica ferry stop (the one before the Accademia), walks along the passageway to the small square where one can go left through portals and toward Accademia, then along that small canal to about the eighth doorway. There are about 26 rooms, all up a tall narrow courtyard staircase. The help took care of all bookings, all stamps, etc. There is a fine breakfast room and a garden in the rear is being rebuilt - for dining I think. Our rooms were on the canal itself. The best thing is that we felt like residents: no tourists in sight."

Hotel Gabbia d'Oro, Miss Camille Balfarro, Corso Portoni Borsari 4/A, 37121 Verona, Italy; tel: (045) 8003060; fax: (045) 590293; 27 rooms: Lire 270,000-460,000; *Recommended by Virginia Clements, Beverly Hills, California*

Of all the hotel recommendations we have recently received, none has been more welcome than the Hotel Gabbia d'Oro in Verona - it looks like a perfect gem. "We visited a new hotel which has been open for 10 months. We saw the common rooms, and they are charming, clean, and give an olde worlde feeling. The manager couldn't have been nicer. She showed us around her peaceful and quiet domain, giving us all the time we wanted, even knowing we would not be staying at the hotel (regretfully)." Note: After looking at the brochure of the Hotel Gabbia d'Oro, we must admit it looks superb: beautifully decorated with antiques, cozy, charming and absolutely inviting. We can hardly wait to see it ourselves.

HOTEL RESERVATION REQUEST LETTER IN ITALIAN

HOTEL NAME & ADDRESS - clearly printed or typed

Vi prego di voler riservare: I would like to request:

_____   *Numero delle camere con bagno o doccia privata*
Number of rooms with private bath or shower

_____   *Numero delle camere senza bagno o doccia*
Number of rooms without private bath or shower

_____   *Data di arrivo*   _____   *Data di Partenza*
Date of arrival   Date of departure

Vi prego inoltre de fornirmi le seguenti informazioni:
Please let me know as soon as possible the following:

Potete riservare le camere richieste?	*SI*	*NO*
Can you reserve the space requested?	yes	no
Prezzo giornaliero _____		
Price per night		
I pasti sono compresi nel prezzo?	*SI*	*NO*
Are meals included in your rate?	yes	no
E necessario un deposito?	SI	NO
Do you need a deposit?	yes	no

Quanto e necessario come deposito?   _____
How much deposit do you need?

Ringraziando anticipatamente, porgo distinti saluti,
Thanking you in advance, I send my best regards,

YOUR NAME & ADDRESS - clearly printed or typed

Index - Alphabetically by Hotel & Town

Index of Hotels and Towns

Index of Hotels and Towns

DISCOVERIES FROM OUR READERS

"Discoveries from Our Readers" features places to stay that sound excellent, but which we have not yet had an opportunity to visit. If you have a favorite hideaway that you would be willing to share with other readers, we would love to hear from you. The type of accommodations we feature are those with old world ambiance, special charm, and warmth of welcome. Please send the following information:

1. *Your name, address and telephone number.*

2. *Name, address and telephone number of your discovery.*

3. *Rate for a double room including tax, service and breakfast.*

4. *Brochure or picture (we cannot return material).*

5. *Permission to use an edited version of your description.*

6. *Would you want your name, city, and state included in the book?*

Please send to:

Karen Brown's Country Inn Guides, Post Office Box 70, San Mateo, CA 94401, USA
Telephone (415) 342-5591   Fax (415) 342-9153

Karen Brown's Country Inn Guides

The Most Reliable Series on Charming Places to Stay

KAREN BROWN'S
FRENCH
Country Inns & Itineraries

UPDATED AND REVISED • SIXTH EDITION

KAREN BROWN'S
CALIFORNIA
Country Inns & Itineraries

UPDATED AND REVISED • SECOND EDITION

KAREN BROWN'S
ITALIAN
Country Inns & Itineraries

UPDATED AND REVISED • FOURTH EDITION

KAREN BROWN'S
FRENCH
Country Bed & Breakfasts

UPDATED AND REVISED • SECOND EDITION

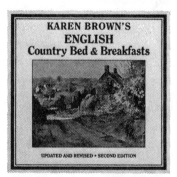

KAREN BROWN'S
ENGLISH
Country Bed & Breakfasts

UPDATED AND REVISED • SECOND EDITION

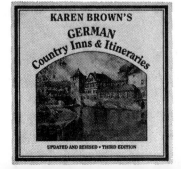

KAREN BROWN'S
GERMAN
Country Inns & Itineraries

UPDATED AND REVISED • THIRD EDITION

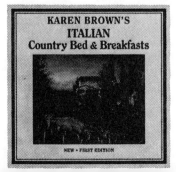

KAREN BROWN'S
ITALIAN
Country Bed & Breakfasts

NEW • FIRST EDITION

KAREN BROWN'S
ENGLISH, WELSH & SCOTTISH
Country Hotels & Itineraries

UPDATED AND REVISED • SIXTH EDITION

Order Form

KAREN BROWN'S COUNTRY INN GUIDES

Please ask in your local bookstore for **KAREN BROWN'S COUNTRY INN** guides.
If the books you want are unavailable, you may order directly from the publisher.

_____ *Austrian Country Inns & Castles (1988 edition) $6.00*
_____ *California Country Inns & Itineraries $14.95*
_____ *English Country Bed & Breakfasts $13.95*
_____ *English, Welsh & Scottish Country Hotels & Itineraries $14.95*
_____ *French Country Bed & Breakfasts $13.95*
_____ *French Country Inns & Itineraries $14.95*
_____ *German Country Inns & Itineraries $14.95*
_____ *Irish Country Inns (1988 edition) $6.00*
_____ *Italian Country Bed & Breakfasts $13.95*
_____ *Italian Country Inns & Itineraries $14.95*
_____ *Portuguese Country Inns & Pousadas $12.95*
_____ *Scandinavian Country Inns & Manors   (1987 edition) $6.00*
_____ *Spanish Country Inns & Paradors $12.95*
_____ *Swiss Country Inns & Chalets   (1989 edition) $6.00*

Name _____   Street _____

City _____   State _____   Zip _____   tel: _____

Credit Card (Mastercard or Visa) _____   Exp: _____

Add $3.50 for the first book and .50 for each additional book for postage & packing.
California residents add 8.25% sales tax.
Indicate number of copies of each title; send form with check or credit card information to:

KAREN BROWN'S COUNTRY INN GUIDES
Post Office Box 70, San Mateo, California, 94401, U.S.A.
Tel: (415) 342-9117   Fax: (415) 342-9153

Karen Brown's
Italian Country Bed & Breakfasts

Bed & Breakfast Travel in Italy

The Latest and Delightfully Inexpensive Way
To Experience the Italian Countryside

Italian Country Bed & Breakfasts was written as a companion guide to Karen Brown's *Italian Country Inns & Itineraries*. Bed & Breakfast accommodation is a relatively new trend in Italy and this is the first guide ever written that has "hand-picked" the very best of the places to stay. All the pertinent information is given: description of the accommodation, sketch, price, driving directions, level of English spoken, what meals are served, name of the owner, telephone number, dates open, etc.

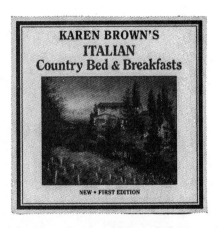

KAREN BROWN'S
ITALIAN
Country Bed & Breakfasts

NEW • FIRST EDITION

Italian Country Bed & Breakfast does not replace *Italian Country Inns & Itineraries*, but together they make the perfect pair for the traveller who wants to explore the countryside of Italy. Both feature places to stay with charm, warmth of welcome and old world ambiance: *Italian Country Inns & Itineraries* includes hotels and small inns, *Italian Country Bed & Breakfasts* has places to stay in private homes. The Bed & Breakfasts are located throughout Italy and offer an intriguing selection of accommodation from rustic Tuscan farmhouses and enchanting stone cottages to gracious country villas. This is an opportunity to meet Italians in their homes - almost like being a guest where you are welcomed like a friend of the family.

KAREN BROWN wrote her first travel guide, French Country Inns & Chateaux, in 1979. This original guide is now in its 6th edition plus 13 books have been added to the series which has become known as the most personalized, reliable reference library for the discriminating traveller. Although Karen's staff has expanded, she is still involved in the publication of her guide books. Karen, her husband, Rick, their daughter, Alexandra, and son, Richard, live on the coast south of San Francisco at their own country inn, Seal Cove Inn, in Moss Beach, California.

CLARE BROWN, CTC, has many years of experience in the field of travel and has earned the designation of Certified Travel Consultant. Since 1969 she has specialized in planning itineraries to Europe using charming small hotels in the countryside for her clients. The focus of her job remains unchanged, but now her expertise is available to a larger audience - the readers of her daughter's Country Inn guides. Clare lives in the San Francisco Bay area with her husband, Bill.

BARBARA TAPP, the talented artist responsible for all of the hotel sketches and delightful illustrations in this guide, was raised in Australia where she studied in Sydney at the School of Interior Design. Although Barbara continues with freelance projects, she devotes much of her time to illustrating Karen's Country Inn guides. Barbara lives in the San Francisco Bay area with her husband, Richard, their two sons, Jonothan and Alexander, and young daughter, Georgia.

JANN POLLARD, the artist responsible for the beautiful painting on the cover of this guide, has studied art since childhood, and is well-known for her outstanding impressionistic-style water colors which she has exhibited in numerous juried shows, winning many awards. Jann travels frequently to Europe (using Karen Brown's guides) where she loves to paint old world archi-tecture. Jann lives in the San Francisco Bay area with her husband, Gene, and their two daughters.

SEAL COVE INN - LOCATED IN THE SAN FRANCISCO AREA

Karen (Brown) Herbert is best known as a writer and publisher of the Karen Brown's Country Inn guides, favorites of travellers searching for the most charming country inns throughout Europe and California. Now Karen and her husband, Rick, have put sixteen years of experience into reality and opened their own superb hideaway, Seal Cove Inn. Spectacularly set amongst wildflowers and bordered by towering cypress trees, Seal Cove Inn looks out to the ocean over acres of county park: an oasis where you can enjoy secluded beaches, explore tide-pools, watch frolicking seals, and follow the tree-lined path tracing the windswept ocean bluffs. Country antiques, lovely original watercolors, flower-filled cradles, rich fabrics, and the gentle ticking of grandfather clocks create the perfect ambiance for a foggy day in front of the crackling log fire. Each bedroom is its own private haven with a comfortable sitting area before a wood-burning fireplace and doors opening onto a private patio with views to the distant ocean. Moss beach is a 30-minute drive south of San Francisco, 6 miles north of the picturesque town of Half Moon Bay, and a few minutes from Princeton harbor with its colorful fishing boats and restaurants. Seal Cove Inn makes a perfect base for whale-watching expeditions, salmon-fishing excursions, day trips to San Francisco, exploring the coast, or, best of all, just a romantic interlude by the sea - time to relax and be pampered. Karen and Rick are looking forward to meeting and welcoming you to their own inn.

Seal Cove Inn, 221 Cypress Avenue, Moss Beach, California, 94038, U.S.A.
telephone: (415) 728-7325   fax: (415) 728-4116